D1435389

The
Dream-Working
Handbook

THIS IS A CARLTON BOOK
Design copyright © Carlton Books Limited 2001
Text copyright © Helen McLean and Abiye Cole 2001

This edition published by Carlton Books Limited 2001
20 Mortimer Street
London
W1N 7RD

A CIP catalogue record for this book is available from the
British Library.

ISBN 1 84222 117 5

Design: Sue Clarke
Cover Design: Alison Tutton

Printed in the United Kingdom

Helen McLean & Abiye Cole

The
Dream-Working
Handbook

Learn to

Understand

the Personal

Significance

of Your

Dreams

CONTENTS

INTRODUCTION

Long ago, when the world was young, an old Lakota spiritual leader on a high mountain had a vision. In his vision, Iktomi, the great trickster and teacher of wisdom, appeared in the form of a spider. Iktomi spoke in a sacred language, and while doing so, picked up the old man's willow hoop, which had feathers, horsehair, beads and offerings attached to it, and began to spin a web.

He spoke to the old man about the cycles of life – how we begin our lives as infants, move on through childhood and into adulthood, finally reaching old age, where we must be taken care of like infants again, thus completing the life cycle. "But," said Iktomi, as he continued to spin his web, "in each time of life there are many forces, some good and some bad. If you listen to the good forces, they will steer you in the right direction. But if you listen to the bad forces, they will steer you in the wrong direction and may hurt you. So these forces can help or can hinder the harmony of nature."

While speaking, the spider continued to weave his web. When he finished speaking, Iktomi gave the old man the web and said, "The web is a perfect circle with a hole in the centre. Use it to help your people reach their goals, making good use of their ideas, dreams and visions. If you believe in the great spirit, the web will catch your good ideas and the bad ones will go through the hole."

The old man described his vision to others, and now many Native Americans hang a dream-catcher above their bed to sift their dreams and visions. The good is captured in the web of life and carried with the people, but the evil in their dreams drops through the hole in the centre and is no longer part of their lives. It is said that the dream-catcher holds the seeds of possibility for the future.

The origins of Dream Catchers

A dream-catcher is a Native American artefact believed to have originated with the Oneida people of the northeastern United States. It is said to filter and retain good dreams while allowing bad ones to disappear. A dream-catcher consists of a wooden hoop over which a web of thin hide is stretched. Beads and feathers are attached to it for added beauty and charm. Dream-catchers are often given to infants and children so that their dreams may come true. They are kept throughout the owner's life and their power increases with use.

The Dream Catchers organization works in a similar way. We can teach you to use dream-catching to enjoy and retain the positive messages contained in your dreams. You will learn how to let go of negative feelings and move on. Your dream-catching skills will continue to develop throughout your life. The more they are employed, the more empowered you will become.

How to use this book

The Dream Catchers Handbook invites you to get to work on your dreams immediately. It does not have to be read right through – you can select the sections that are appropriate to your needs and then refer to other parts as necessary.

If this is the first time you have considered the importance of dreams, you will probably find it useful to read the first three chapters to give you some background and historical information. Should you want to look at the historical aspect of dreams in more detail, you will find a list of recommended reading at the end of the book.

If you have already tried to work out your dreams by referring to dream dictionaries or other manuals, or if you are impatient to work on a particular dream, you can go straight to Chapter 4 and begin catching your dream. It is important to apply all the dream-catching steps outlined there. Then you can let your imagination run free. This is the cornerstone of effective dream-catching, and will eventually become second nature.

Work through each dream in as much detail as you require. If you have difficulty getting past some point in the working, refer to the troubleshooting exercises outlined in Chapter 9. You can also call Dream Catchers Dreamline (see page 186) if you would like to work through your dream with one of our professionals and have the process demonstrated.

You will certainly get a lot out of your first attempts at dream-working, but you should be aware that dream-catching is a skill developed through practice. The more you work on your dreams, the more illuminating they become.

Although you will gain a great deal from following the self-help steps within this book, attending a lecture demonstration or weekend workshop will make

the whole process come alive. Through observing the work of a practised dream-catcher, you cannot help but become inspired to go further into the process yourself. Witnessing others working through their dreams, and then practising the method yourself will give you the confidence to apply what you have learned to your own dreams. ☆

1

DREAM-CATCHING FOR BEGINNERS

"There once was a man who dreamt
he was a butterfly. The experience
was so deep and so real that
upon waking he could not be
sure if it was a dream.
Perhaps now he was a butterfly
dreaming he was a man?"

TAO TE CHING BY LAO-ZSU (6TH CENTURY BC)

Everyone dreams. Whether we remember them or not, dreams have more than a trivial connection to our waking life. Most of us have experienced waking from a powerful dream with images that have stayed with us throughout the day, perhaps lingering in our memory for years. We dream up strange, sometimes disjointed, often nonsensical images in order to process the many impressions we gather and have to screen out while going about our daily activities. Within this mass of information there are nuggets of knowledge, feeling and creativity that we might overlook because they are wrapped in code and we are just too busy to give them attention.

If we don't manage to access our dreams, or if we persistently resist their messages, they may grow heavier and more exaggerated until they burst upon us in forms too disturbing to ignore. Nightmares wake us up to some aspect of our lives that needs attention. The same is true of recurring dreams. When worked upon and understood, nightmares disappear and recurring dreams begin to change until they too fade away. Dreams process our practical and emotional concerns while we sleep, and can become a great support within our lives.

The dream-catching process can encourage us to let go and move on when we feel stuck, help us to make decisions, and enable us to heal after loss and betrayal. Dreams can show us how to bring more joy and laughter into our lives, and they often provide inspirational solutions for our professional and artistic endeavours.

Introduction to gestalt

This handbook is the culmination of many years of gestalt dream-working. Gestalt is a psychological term meaning a whole that is perceived as greater than the sum of its parts. The gestalt way of working recognizes that when something is unfinished or incomplete within a person's life, there is a striving for completion. Just as most people would try to slot the last pieces into an incomplete jigsaw, so most of us seek to resolve or at least come to terms with unsatisfactory situations.

Helen first came across the gestalt way of working with dreams in the early 1970s when she participated in a gestalt group. There she witnessed a seventy-year-old woman working through a dream that had puzzled her. As the dreamer identified with the dream's images and freely associated with the events in it as if they were happening in the present, she became filled with feeling and began to weep quietly. She then explained that her two-year-old sister had died when she herself was six, and her family – in an attempt to block out the pain they were all feeling – had never talked about it. Consequently, she had not been given the opportunity to cry. Now, reliving this dream, a chord had been struck that resurrected her grief and at last she could let go and cry for the little sister who had been such a big part of her life. Even though her feelings felt as fresh as when they were first tucked away, they were now more bearable, for she was no longer that small child, and no longer alone. She had the assistance of a gestalt practitioner and the support of the group to encourage her to release herself from the control she'd had to exercise in order to suppress her grief. As she spoke gratefully of her dream, her relief was apparent. It was as if she had been released from a silent prison.

Feelings may be put away, but they do not go away. They remain a suppressed dynamic force waiting to emerge at any opportunity. Withheld feelings can be triggered by unexpected events that resonate with previous longings, losses and betrayals. Dreams allow feelings to flow freely, processing not only the unfinished business of the past twenty-four hours, but also the stored-up business of a lifetime. This can be both a relief and a worry. Even if you are unaware of the workings of your dreams, they themselves will be working to find solutions for your dilemmas.

Nowadays, there is a general recognition that many illnesses are exacerbated, if not caused, by the stress of repressed feelings. The worry, tension and energy we put into dealing with or avoiding difficult relationships and provocative situations can cost us a lot. We mentally rehearse important encounters in the hope of controlling the outcome, only to be thwarted by other people's responses and our own unscripted surges of emotion. Feelings will out, and it takes a great deal of energy to hold them in.

After participating in her first workshop, Helen was deeply impressed by the potency of gestalt dream-work and realized for the first time the power and importance of being able to express feelings safely. She was thrilled by the possibility of gaining access to her unconscious processes through dreams, and remembers how she immediately started to practise basic dream-working skills with a friend who was sharing her home at the time. "We would regularly tell each other our dreams over our breakfast tea, giggling and sometimes weeping at their significance. Our dreams invited us to own disowned parts of ourselves, our joys as well as our sorrows. They gave us the experience of opening our hearts as well as our minds. We felt encouraged to live in the expectation of joy rather than fear. And they showed us that we were bigger, more powerful, more beautiful and freer than we had imagined. Through attending further workshops and practising with my friend, I no longer felt as if my life was totally driven by forces out of my control. I was starting to understand and look after myself in a way I had never been able to before. I could now recognize and begin to face the facts of my life. I was also seeing the creative solutions that were being offered to me through my dreaming."

After attending several workshops, Helen considered embarking on a training course to become a gestalt practitioner. She knew this was a big step to take and wasn't confident that she could afford the course fees or that she would be capable of doing the work well. When the selection weekend arrived, she was no nearer to making her decision. Then she remembered a recent dream.

"I was at Cambridge railway station and I had the choice of two trains – a great trans-American one steaming at the platform, or the usual suburban train heading for London. Through exploring the dream, I came to realize that the trains related to the real-life training choices I was facing, and I found the courage to commit myself to doing the course I liked." (The process of working through this dream is described in more detail in Chapter 5.)

Helen has continued to have significant dreams. "My dreaming has opened up personal opportunities, enabling me to make the most of resources and skills I might not have recognized. I can map many important adult milestones with the titles of dreams I have worked through. In times of stress and difficulty, my dreams have invited me to face facts that I have been trying to avoid, that I would rather not deal with."

Occasionally a dream will sweep into consciousness with such force or vitality that we cannot help but pay attention to it. Waking trembling, sweating or suffused with feeling, it may take some time to recognize that we have been dreaming. Slowly we review our experience and realize that the dream has profoundly changed our perspective. These dreams usually come to us unbidden, often at times when the opportunity or necessity for change is upon us.

ELEPHANT DREAM

Helen had been living in France for some time and it was just such a dream that woke her up to the fact that she had no option but to return to England.

"In the dream I can see that there is a very emaciated, weak-looking elephant standing unsteadily in the field [among the horses]. *I know the elephant needs food and water, so I go to the stables to collect the hay barrow and find that it has shrunk to just a narrow trough full of little boxes, jars and other oddments. I start to sort out these bits and pieces, putting them on shelves and tidying them away. I wake up without having fed the elephant, and feeling dreadful and somewhat disturbed."*

When working through the dream later, she identified with the elephant, saying:
"I am a large, withered, grey wrinkly creature and I need to be fed."
(She was starting menopause and could really identify with this description!)

She also said:
"I am in a country that is not my own. I can't speak the language and although I can get on with these horses, they are not of my own kind. But I can survive here as long as I am fed."

The elephant was Helen, of course. She had desperately wanted to stay in France, even though her resources were dwindling and work prospects were not good. But this dream brought home to her how difficult it had been to survive over the previous months. She was facing the fact that she couldn't earn her living in France. She was running out of savings and missing the company of close friends. Working through this dream enabled her to accept that living in France was no longer viable, that she was feeling alienated and hungry for her "own kind". She looked towards England and found the courage to return.

As it turned out, returning gave her a new lease of life both professionally and emotionally. She says: "Whenever I have worked through a dream, acknowledging the truth of it as a reflection of my life, I have been enabled to move on. I have felt the relief of knowing and found the courage (at times tinged with sadness) to do what I know has to be done. The emotional impact of this dream and the directness of the dream elephant's message brought home to me how important it is to pay attention to dreams. It struck me that although uncovering the wisdom within dreams is a fairly straightforward process, not many people have yet learned to do it for themselves."

This thought led us to set up Dream Catchers in order to teach and support those who want to decipher their own dreams. One of the chapters of the *I Ching* (the Chinese Book of Changes) is entitled *Hsu* – which literally means "waiting". It makes the following observation: "It's only when we have the courage to face the facts exactly as they are without any self-deception or illusion that a light will appear out of events by which the way forward will be shown."

This quote encapsulates the process of both gestalt and dream-catching. We know that within every dream there is a kernel of truth that will throw light upon a situation, revealing both the difficulty and the way through. Sometimes a dream will bring a joyful message, encouraging the dreamer to take a risk and reach out to life, showing them aspects of themselves that their own modesty or lack of self-esteem have not allowed them to own. Working through dreams can provide much amusement and spontaneous drama for the dreamer, as well as for those who witness the process of the dream message being "brought home". Dreams often pun, offering unexpected insights through the richness of their imagery and the language the dreamer may use to describe them. They can also offer comfort and consolation during times of disillusionment or suffering.

Solace through dreaming

During one of Helen's regular guest appearances on a radio phone-in, a woman called in great distress, saying that she was very unhappy because her beloved cat, Pixie, had died. She felt inconsolable and for several months had been able to do little but think of her beloved pet. She said that people, including a counsellor, did try to help her, but to no avail.

Helen asked the woman if she had a dream about Pixie. She replied that she had, and described a dream in which Pixie had come back, jumped up on the bed and had snuggled down close to her, just as always. The dream had been so real that the woman had said, "Oh, Pixie, why did you go away? Please don't leave me again." She had then reached out to touch the cat, only to waken and realize it was a dream. The caller then wept bitterly, saying that she didn't know how she would get over this loss and that she longed to die herself as she could see no reason to live any more.

Helen asked her to imagine what Pixie would say if she knew how unhappy she was. The woman said she knew Pixie had loved her and that she wouldn't want her to be so unhappy. Her voice changed a little at this point, becoming less hurt, a little clearer. She then said, "But I'm haunted by how Pixie died. She had such a terrible death that I can't get it out of my mind."

Helen asked her how Pixie was when she had appeared in her dream and the woman replied, "She was perfect, just like before the accident."

Helen invited the woman to remember Pixie in that way – the way she had appeared in her dream. The caller quietened and could take a little comfort from this suggestion. There was still a long way to go but her dream had given her an image that not only spoke to her suffering but also confirmed that her beloved pet would not wish her to suffer in this way. By catching the underlying message of her dream, the woman was comforted.

Anybody can learn to dream-catch. For most of her professional life Helen has worked within the specialized field of therapy and training, which gives only a small proportion of the population access to their dream messages. Her regular radio phone-in indicates that there are vast numbers of people who are curious about their dreams, and capable of gaining help and support from them. Most of these listeners do not need, and would never think of using, counselling or therapy.

Dream Catchers invite dreamers to be playful – to use free association (allowing their thoughts and feelings to arise uncensored). In this way they become open to the new perspectives, possibilities and creative solutions held within their dreams.

Dream-catching facts
- All dreams, even nightmares and recurring dreams, contain supportive messages for the dreamer.
- Dream-catching offers those who want to know an inside line to their inner truths.
- Confused or conflict-ridden life situations can be resolved when dreams are listened to.
- Sticking-points and resistances can be creatively worked through by asking your subconscious for a dream and working with it.
- Dreams often reveal more about personal resources and the potentials for success than a dreamer may be consciously aware of.
- Dreams can alert you to your emotional and physical needs.
- Dreams often warn dreamers to pay attention to their personal safety, health and well-being.

The power and logic of dreams

We have found that intellectual or cognitive explanations of dreams are pale substitutes for active dream-working. Talking about and analysing a dream misses most of the vitality and all the fun of active dream-catching. It's like watching characters on black and white television when you could be actively taking up the opportunities offered by your own life.

It is possible to witness the point where dreamers first connect with the importance of their dreams. In the midst of talking or explaining, they will pause, flush, laugh or even go pale. They are momentarily silent as they take on the significance of the dream-work and connect with the truth of it. They may be so startled that they barely pause, rushing to complete their explanations, hardly daring to believe what the dream has told them. At this point they will be encouraged to slow down and fully comprehend the new perspective that has been offered to them. A dream-catcher might ask, "What happened there a moment ago?" Then, when the dreamers give themselves permission to believe the evidence of their own emotional responses, they can allow themselves to explore new possibilities and believe that there are other ways forward.

A journalist who had been researching different methods of dream-working recently brought Helen a dream that she had already been working on with a therapist from another discipline. Five minutes into the session, the journalist caught her breath and paused, looking startled. "This is so powerful," she said with her hand on her midriff, "I can actually feel what is going on."

At the end of the session she felt she had intellectually got to much the same point she had reached in her session with the first therapist. However, through the dream-catching process (when she let herself work the dream in the present and really feel the impact of what she was saying and doing), significant connections had come flooding into her mind. As a result, she felt lighter and considerably relieved. She now understood through the dream not just her present situation, but that an old hurt was still having a restrictive influence upon her life. Several weeks later she telephoned Helen to say that the significance of the dream had stayed with her and she had felt able to make some life-changing decisions.

Of course, the work the journalist did with Helen was "on the shoulders" of the work she had done before, but her experience within the dream session was one that Helen is used to witnessing. Her response was like that of many clients, who have "come to their senses" via the three-dimensional impact of dream-catching.

This handbook demonstrates a simple yet effective way of working with dreams that will enable you to unlock your dream wisdom for yourself. In fact, it will enable you to start working on your dreams immediately in a powerful and fascinatingly personal way. Its inspiration comes from the collective experience of the Dream Catchers organization, an educational body that has been established in order to teach people how to access the uniquely personal wisdom contained within their dreams.

While dream dictionaries can be interesting on a superficial level, their use cannot help but miss the essential meaning that your personal dream symbols will have for you. The vital messages contained within dreams can only be fully understood when dreamers re-immerse themselves within their dreams and investigate for themselves the significance that the dreams have within the context of their life. The true essence of dream catching is interaction, exploration and discovery. This handbook illustrates the method by giving examples of actual dreams being worked through, along with the insights and benefits they have offered their dreamers.

You will be guided step by step through a straightforward process that will reconnect you to your dream. Once you have done this, you will be able to explore your dream at your own pace, picking up its messages and identifying with its emotional content in a way that will enable you to make connections with your current life situation. Should you encounter any difficulty in engaging with or understanding any part of your dream, you can also get live support on the telephone or Internet from one of our team of experienced dream-catchers.

This opportunity to experience the dream-catching process and have the objective support of a professional dream-worker will be invaluable to novices and experienced dream-workers alike. ✩

2

AN HISTORICAL PERSPECTIVE

Accounts of dreaming through the ages can be found in a multitude of dream books, so rather than providing a comprehensive history of dreams in this chapter, we have selected a few examples that illustrate the special place that dreams have held for mankind throughout the ages. If you wish to look more deeply into the history of dreams, you will find some recommended further reading at the end of the book.

Dreaming in ancient cultures

Dreams have an importance that spans time as well as geographical and cultural boundaries. Here we offer a brief glimpse of how various civilizations and cultures have used dream wisdom. Given that non-literate cultures across the world have strong traditions of dream interpretation, it is safe to assume that human beings have been looking at dreams in some form or other since we first tried to make sense of our existence. Some scholars have theorized that in early societies it was the experience of dreaming, plus the recognition that in dreams anything is possible, that led to a belief in parallel universes, perhaps even the concept of life after death. The experience of dreaming is so like stepping into another world that it could well have inspired the ancients to recognize the spirit as separable from the body. That early conception of spirituality might have provided the seeds for religion as we know it today. All the beliefs and dream-working methods that have followed since suggest that dreams are a pathway to some form of enlightenment.

MESOPOTAMIA

The first records we have of dream interpretation came from Mesopotamia, a civilization dating back to 5000 BC and the first to leave written evidence of religious beliefs. The Mesopotamians left us the world's first dream book, a compilation of dream symbols and their meanings, which, although incomplete, testifies to the place dreaming was given in this ancient culture. Dreams were seen as omens sent by the gods to indicate the future. They were interpreted by a specialist priest, or a priest could be asked to have an enlightening dream on a supplicant's behalf. It is thought that dream incubation, a process of encouraging dreams through special rituals within dedicated temples, was invented at this time. This practice then spread throughout much of the ancient world, surviving in some form or other until the beginning of the twentieth century. It is believed that the Mesopotamian model for dream interpretation spread throughout Egypt and formed the basis of Hebrew, Arab and Greek dream traditions.

ANCIENT EGYPT

The Egyptians, although inheriting many of their ideas from Mesopotamia, developed a different belief system, with dreams playing a smaller part. They also had dream dictionaries and saw dreams as messages sent from various divinities. Temples were dedicated to Serapis, the Egyptian god of dreams, and resident dream interpreters helped to develop the process of dream incubation. Those seeking answers would perform rituals, make sacrifices, say prayers and sleep within the grounds of the temple in the hope of receiving a dream that would reveal their future. The pharaoh's dreams were accorded the utmost importance because he himself was viewed as a god; given his status, it also seemed natural that the gods would be more likely to communicate important dreams through him.

ANCIENT GREECE

Around 335 BC the Greek philosopher Aristotle claimed that human beings are capable of achieving a pure form of wisdom when our minds are given free rein during sleep. Ancient Greece was then the most powerful civilization on Earth, and the font of its wisdom was the oracle at Delphi, a central part of Greek culture, which even influenced important government decisions. What is less well known is that pronouncements of the oracle were based on dreams. Never since then have dreams affected the world in such a momentous way. They exerted a huge influence on military and domestic policies, and helped shape the ancient world. The Greek system of dream interpretation was not concerned with merely foretelling the future: it was also used to improve the general well-being of the dreamer. Aesculapius, a doctor who used dreams extensively in his consultations, was such a success that he was deified and hundreds of dream temples were constructed in his honour. His influence was so strong that he also became a popular Roman god and continued to be worshipped until around 800 years after his death.

Hippocrates, accepted as the founder of modern medicine, saw dreams as important indicators of the physical and mental health of the patient. This was perhaps the first realization that dreams are not necessarily from a divine

21

source, but can bring messages to the dreamer from the inner self.

Ancient Greece is also the source of one of the most influential dream books ever written. The *Oneirocritica* ("The Interpretation of Dreams") by Artemidorus still forms the basis of many modern dream dictionaries.

ANCIENT ROME
Roman dream tradition borrowed very heavily on that of the Greeks. It is said that Julius Caesar's successor, Augustus, believed so strongly in the prophetic nature of dreams that he created a law compelling any citizen who had a dream about the empire to announce it in the market-place. There are also accounts of rulers justifying unpopular policies to the public by claiming that they were revealed in important dreams. The significance of dreams was hotly debated in Rome, with many scholars (of whom Cicero was the most vocal) openly claiming that dreams were inspired by our own passions, emotions and day-to-day experiences rather than by divine forces.

Dreams and religion
Significance has been given to dreams throughout history, and religious dream interpretation has inevitably had an impact on our present-day attitude to dreams. As Umberto Eco wrote in *The Name of the Rose* (1980), "A dream is a scripture, and many scriptures are nothing but dreams."

JUDAISM
"An uninterpreted dream is like an unopened letter," said Rabbi Hisda (*c.* 250-309). The Talmud, the ancient book of Jewish faith and law compiled from writings by eminent rabbinical scholars, contains a number of guidelines for interpreting dreams and advice on how to avoid "evil" dreams. A strong distinction was made between the good and evil varieties. Although all divine dreams were believed to come from God, the existence of symbolic dreams was also acknowledged.

Judaism stressed that dream interpretation required great skill and that only gifted Jews were able to interpret symbolic dreams accurately. (In the Old Testament only Jews such as Joseph and Daniel are able to interpret dreams correctly.) Talmudic writings demonstrate a variety of opinions about symbolic dreams and methods for interpreting them. Some of these have much in common with modern methods of dream interpretation. For example, some writers stressed that to arrive at an accurate understanding of a dream, it was vital to consider the personal circumstances of the dreamer – his temperament, the nature of his vocation and his mood at the time of the dream.

CHRISTIANITY

"We do not sleep merely to live, but to learn to live well," said the fifth-century bishop Synesius. When the apostle Peter dreamt three times of clean and unclean animals, it marked an important turning-point for Christianity in its transformation from a Jewish sect into a universal religion. The New Testament has far fewer dream events than the Old Testament, and Christianity's attitude to dreams has varied widely throughout its history. The Bible records that God spoke directly to some through dreams. Many saints and important religious figures experienced significant dreams that led them to great religious acts. It was also widely believed that just as God could send dreams for the good of mankind, so the devil could poison minds with false and malevolent dreams. Given the strict moral code of the time, it is understandable that dreams often featured taboo subjects or "unholy" acts (things that now, in post-Freudian times, are considered unremarkable). Such dreams were ascribed to evil forces.

During the sexual and political repression of the Middle Ages and at the time of the Inquisition, we can imagine the terror and the shame that must have been felt by the clergy and the righteous when they experienced (quite normal) dreams of a sexual nature. They were not to know that the repression of sexuality inevitably leads to sexual dreams. The Church explained unholy dreams by the invention of succubi and incubi – demons capable of assuming pleasing forms that could seduce and sometimes even impregnate dreamers (an expedient way of accepting "immoral" thoughts and illicit liaisons). This formed part of the newer theological thinking that an individual could not be accountable for sins committed in their dreams, in the same way that they could not expect to enter heaven for good thoughts rather than good acts.

Synesius, one of the few senior Church figures actively to encourage the study of dreams, was far ahead of his time both in his advice about keeping a dream journal and in his warnings on the use of dream dictionaries. Even then he was aware that the significance of particular dreams and symbols differed from one dreamer to another.

ISLAM

"Now Allah has created the dream not only as a means of guidance and instruction…but he has made it a window on the Unseen." There was already a tradition of dream interpretation in the Arab world before the Prophet Muhammad (c. 570–632) spoke these words, but it soon had an impact that was unparalleled in any other religion. Not only did Muhammad have his own destiny revealed to him in a dream, but much of the Koran, Islam's holy book, was dictated to him through dreams. One of Muhammad's most important experiences is related in the famous "Night Journey", an account of a dream in which he meets God, Jesus and the other prophets, and the mysteries of the cosmos are revealed to him. Muhammad encouraged his disciples to relate their dreams each morning, when he would interpret them and share his own.

The Islamic faith separated dreams into different types in a way similar to the Hebrew tradition. It distinguished "true" dreams, which featured God, Muhammad or angels, and "bad" dreams, which featured demons or came from what were seen as our personal desires and preoccupations.

HINDUISM

The Hindu view of dreams has much in common with those of many other cultures, including the belief that dreams occur when the soul leaves the body and voyages to other realms. During the Vedic period (c. 1500–500 BC) dreams were seen as good or bad omens, and some writings offer guidance about how to interpret the symbols within them. The Atharva Veda features a whole treatise on dreams and includes a number of ideas that still hold true for the way in which we understand dreams today. For example, it suggests that unremembered dreams are not significant, and that dreams may be influenced by certain types of food, illness or our desires. Some Hindu writings even describe our existence on this planet as being like a dream in its unpredictability: it is a dream from which we can wake only when we achieve true enlightenment. Hindu theology later considered that dreams were a manifestation of a sixth sense, a kind of intuition, since the other senses were thought to be inactive during sleep.

BUDDHISM

Although evolved from the Hindu religion, Buddhism hardly exists at all now in India, and dreams have never been central to its philosophy. However, they do feature prominently in Buddhist texts. In Tibetan Buddhism, dreams are seen as indicators of how well individuals are progressing in their spiritual and emotional life. Dreams are believed to come from benevolent deities or demons, "bad" dreams being messages that the dreamer must improve certain aspects of his life before the progress he desires can be made.

Tantric (sacred mystical) writings outline techniques used by holy men for "exerting" a dream, in other words creating an artificial dream state which enables them to reach a higher form of meditation or reflection. This type of dream manipulation has much in common with the practice of "lucid dreaming", which is also extensively discussed in the Tantras.

While some branches of religion continue to believe that dream-work has the potential for evil, people of all faiths are nowadays far more likely to decide for themselves how important their dreams are. Dream-catching is based on the premise that each one of us holds the key to unlocking the wisdom of our own dreams.

Dreaming in other non-Western cultures

What we consider to be our modern understanding of dreams is simply an echo of the rich dream heritage developed by ancient civilizations. For many centuries in non-Western cultures the importance of dreams has been widely accepted in ways that we are only now beginning to recognize – despite years of scientific investigation.

SHAMANISM

In many South American and Asian societies, shamans combine the roles of priest, doctor and counsellor. They are the central figures in their social groups, and may be consulted by an individual or the community as a whole, especially when things are going wrong. Shamans have an ability to leave the real world and visit "another reality" – the spirit realm. Whilst there they may communicate with ancestors, fight evil spirits or intercede on behalf of the person(s) consulting them. Dreams form an essential part of shaman life. Indeed, it is through a powerful dream or the delirium of a near-fatal sickness in which they may see their own violent death and rebirth that they recognize their vocation. This experience changes them for ever and enables them to use their dreams to communicate with the spirits and visit the spirit realm, gaining new understanding of specific problems or the likely outcome of events. After a dream journey, shamans are able to prescribe actions to appease the spirits and ensure positive outcomes.

AFRICAN BELIEFS

While the importance of dreams varies widely throughout Africa, there are several shared beliefs, which also have global acceptance. For example, many believe that the soul or spirit leaves the body during dreaming and mingles with the spirits of gods and ancestors.

The Yansi people of Zaire consider dreams to be just as significant as waking experiences. Dreams are interpreted both by elders and medicine men, whose dreams have special significance for the community. The Yansi have their dreams interpreted as soon as they can after waking, believing that the solutions to pressing problems are often to be found within them. Dreams are believed to reveal the deepest worries and desires of an individual, thus helping to explain a person's behaviour within their community. Dreams are also consulted in order to determine the causes of an illness or the likely outcome of a battle or a hunt.

NATIVE AMERICAN BELIEFS

Until the arrival of Westerners, dreams were the only belief system practised by the Iroquois people of North America. They viewed dreams as messengers of the deep desires hidden within a person's soul. They were aware that ignoring these deep-seated feelings could lead to mental or physical illness, and used dream specialists to help decode dreams so that the soul could be given what it required. Each year the Iroquois dedicated a special day for a dramatic and anarchic event called the Ononharoia. During this time the whole community would rush around miming their dreams or relating them in riddles. This practice was believed to be cathartic, allowing the community to understand its dream messages and then to work towards their fulfilment.

The Hopi people saw dreams as the expression of an individual's current life situation, as well as of their place within the community. Whether dreams were seen as good or bad depended on their emotional content. Dreamers were required to discuss bad dreams with the group as a way of exorcising their negativity. (We have adopted the term dream-catching from this tradition.)

Dreams and psychoanalysis

Sigmund Freud (1856-1939) and Carl Jung (1875-1961), the two founding fathers of psychoanalysis, placed great importance on the significance of unconscious processes. "The poets and philosophers before me discovered the unconscious," said Freud. "What I discovered was the scientific method by which the unconscious can be studied."

Freud based much of his life's work on the analysis of his own and his patients' dreams. He uncovered important structures within dreaming and saw them as reflections of how his patients chose to maintain their neuroses. He believed that every dream was a wish, usually related to sexual desire. He also thought that because sexual wishes and fantasies had to be repressed from the consciousness, they surfaced while dreaming. He explained that a dreamer's sexual wishes had to be disguised in order to allay anxiety, so dreams formed in the subconscious translated erotic, forbidden desires into more acceptable, albeit cryptic forms. This process allowed the dreamer to continue sleeping, undisturbed by the severe conflicts and emotions usually felt if such subjects were discussed. Freud later accepted that the hidden material of the dream might also be about guilt or aggression.

There has been a great deal of controversy about – and vilification of – Freud's theories over recent decades, yet few would deny his enormous contribution to our understanding of how the mind works. His book *The Interpretation of Dreams* (1899) shone light on the hidden secrets of a repressive era, exposing the psychological suffering of people unable to express their true selves except through psychosomatic disorder. He too was affected by the mores of his time, and his theories may now be considered passé by some. However, his dedicated mission to make psychology a science has enabled Western society to make huge leaps in its understanding of consciousness.

The narrowness of Freud's interpretations was one of the reasons Carl Jung gave for leaving the Freudian fold. He claimed that Freud's interpretations of his (Jung's) dreams seemed so inadequate that he became determined to follow his own ideas. This led him to investigate what he called the "process of individuation" – a person's journey towards selfhood. In the course of this, he studied some 80,000 dreams, concluding that dreams show a definite progression throughout an individual's life, which corresponded to that person's growth into responsible adulthood. He believed that various transitional points in life were signalled by the appearance of archetypes (recognizable symbols), and if the meanings of these symbols were understood and accepted, a person would be able to negotiate life creatively and soundly. The process of individuation, he believed, could not be willed or controlled, but could certainly be assisted through self-awareness.

Jung believed that modern man lost a great deal when he abandoned his primitive belief in symbols, myths and legends, but that remnants of these "naturalistic" and creative guiding forces were still accessible to us from within the symbolism of dreams. Perhaps one of Jung's most useful ideas for the modern dreamer is the "shadow", an individual's darker side, which may surface in dreams as a threatening or destructive force. If not acknowledged, he believed, the shadow could destroy the individual. Similarly, he believed that when the male (animus) or female (anima) aspect of a personality was denied and suppressed, it would manifest in dreams as a threatening or overpowering the other.

When talking about how his work on dreams differed from Freud's, Jung said that Freud was interested in defining complexes (repressed feelings or thoughts leading to abnormal behaviour or mental states), whereas he wanted to know what the psyche (mind) was doing with these complexes.

Where does this leave us?

From the beginnings of consciousness right up to the present day, the belief has persisted that we can reach wisdom and find solutions to problems through looking at our dreams. The ancients also looked at dreams to give help for the future, believing that it could be shaped by better understanding the present. Dreams allow individuals to confirm and, if necessary, alter the direction of their life. While catching any dream can provide useful insights, the dream that causes a powerful reaction in the dreamer, staying in the mind long after waking, is vitally important to well-being. Such dreams bridge the gap between the sleeping and waking worlds. Their energy exists for a purpose.

The study of dreams over the centuries is yet to produce universal agreement about what they are or what purpose they serve. Our own dream-catching experience confirms our belief that once unravelled, dreams inevitably yield significant information about a dreamer's life, feelings and potential. Gaining access to such knowledge can provide a starting point for improving life and relationships, as well as offering inspiration for a wider good. ☆

3

DREAM FACTS

"I can never decide whether
my dreams are the result of
my thoughts, or my thoughts
the result of my dreams."

D.H. LAWRENCE (1885–1930)

This chapter will give you a basic understanding of the function of dreaming and brief answers to some of the questions most commonly asked. It also includes information about artistic and scientific achievements that have been inspired by dreams. (Those who wish to research the subject of dreams more deeply should refer to the list of further reading at the end of the book.)

What are dreams?

During sleep, the mind relaxes and the consciousness, which has been described as our "window on the world", closes its shutters. This is not to say that the brain stops functioning – it never stops; it is constantly on standby, even when we are unconscious. While our conscious mind rests, the other areas of the mind are given free rein, and it is in these areas that dreams are created. Our worries and desires do not disappear when we sleep. In fact, important feelings and ideas begin to bubble up to the surface. All manner of images and memories of significant people and places, as well as more mundane details from the day, are woven into a weird and wonderful tapestry that comes from deep in our emotional and creative core. The fact that this material is uncensored by our waking mind gives it an integrity which can often reach to the root of our dilemmas.

Without the filter of the rational, conscious mind, our dream stories may be difficult to decipher, yet they contain vital elements of truth and creativity rarely available to us in our waking state. Dream-catching provides a way to reconnect with the primacy of the dream's story, using both the id (the free-flowing creative part of the mind that conjures up the fantastical images and symbols that express our primitive fears and desires) and the rational mind to make sense of the dream.

WHY DO WE DREAM?

Despite a great deal of scientific research, it is still not possible to provide a conclusive answer to this this question. Clinical studies have proved that sleepers prevented from dreaming by being continually woken at the onset of Rapid Eye Movement (REM) sleep – the period when we have the most vivid dreams – are often severely impaired in performing set tasks quickly and accurately. Their stress levels are also heightened and they may show extreme irritability. Dreams evidently provide a very real service for us. It is now widely accepted that finding ways to vent feelings of frustration or dissatisfaction are essential in order for us to maintain well-being. Some Japanese companies invite their employees to vent their spleen on large punch-bags strategically positioned in the workplace. Dreaming allows us metaphorically to do the same thing.

DO WE ALL DREAM?

Everyone dreams, even those who are blind or deaf: their dreams reflect the world as their senses perceive it. Few claim never to have dreamed. However, many of us do find it difficult to remember dreams in detail.

WHY CAN'T I REMEMBER MY DREAMS?

Lack of dream retention can be caused by several factors. You may be waking up during non-REM sleep, which is not the period when vivid dreams occur. You could be blocking out your dreams for fear of confronting the issues that they raise. Being woken by an alarm clock, leaping out of bed too quickly or focusing immediately on the tasks that lie ahead can erase dreams. Certain types of medication, as well as alcohol and drugs, can also affect the ability to remember dreams. Chapter 7 contains advice on how to improve your dream recall, along with some ways to find out for yourself why your dreams are not getting through.

IS IT TRUE THAT DREAMS LAST ONLY A FEW SECONDS?

This is a popular misconception. Dreams timed under clinical conditions have been found to last anything from five to forty-five minutes. Our sense of time is often highly distorted while dreaming, so it is almost impossible to guess how long we have been dreaming in real time.

HOW MANY DREAMS DO WE HAVE PER NIGHT?

During the night we sleep in cycles that range from light to very deep sleep, each one lasting around ninety minutes. Within each of these cycles there will be one period of REM sleep, during which you will experience dreams. Dreams also occur during non-REM sleep, but are far removed from what is normally associated with dreaming – they are closer to normal thought processes and lack the drama and creativity of REM dreams. In studies, test subjects found it almost impossible to recall anything about dreams experienced during non-REM sleep, while those woken during REM sleep were almost always able to recall their dream.

REM dreams are believed to be linked to psychological well-being, while those of non-REM sleep relate to our physical welfare. The average person will have between four and seven dreams per night. While some people may be able to recall several of these, it is more usual to remember only the last dream that occurs just before waking.

ARE DREAMS ALWAYS IN BLACK AND WHITE?

No. Some dreamers experience vivid colours in their dreams, although the prevalence of colour tends to depend on how the dreamer perceives the real world. Artists, for example, have a tendency to notice colours, while others may focus more on ideas. Many dreams take place in an eerie half-light, where colours are quite muted.

IS IT TRUE THAT IF YOU DIE IN YOUR DREAM YOU WON'T WAKE UP?

No. This is a myth. Many individuals have reported experiencing their own death in dreams.

CAN DREAMS PREDICT THE FUTURE?

Just about everybody knows (or knows of) someone who claims to have had a premonitory dream, so they obviously occur. Rather than being entirely new revelations, though, such dreams show that we all know more than we think we do. The brain is gathering and sifting huge amounts of data during the waking day, and some of this may be put in store until it is reactivated and processed by a dream.

Dream Catchers always focus upon the personal significance of a dream for the dreamer, and while we don't discount the possibility of premonitory dreams, we encourage people to discover the significance these dreams have in the present. Like all dreams, those that are powerfully foreboding can usually be understood within the context of a person's experience.

Fearing what seems like a premonitory dream may divert a dreamer from an important message. This will almost certainly have more to do with something currently going on in the dreamer's life than anything that might happen in the future. The present does, of course, affect the future, and dreams could well be warning about the consequences of continuing on a self-destructive path.

WHAT IS LUCID DREAMING?

A lucid dream is one in which the dreamer, although asleep, is aware of dreaming. Some people can even exert control over the outcome of the dream and voluntarily perform actions within it, such as shrinking to miniature size or flying. Lucid dreaming is a fascinating activity and can be useful where dreamers are suffering from particularly disturbing dreams; the ability to take control of events and confront the fearful elements of the dream can rescue them from distress.

The confidence gained through subverting danger and changing events within a dream might then be translated into everyday life. It is possible to train yourself to dream lucidly. Some feel that this ability gains them entry to an elevated state of consciousness. The lucid dreamer is actioning their dreams during sleep in much the same way as dream catchers do when they process their dreams in order to make real life changes.

WHY DO I HAVE THE SAME DREAM OVER AND OVER AGAIN?

Recurring dreams are very common. The fact that a dream keeps returning means that it contains a vital message that needs to be listened to. Such a dream may become more and more exaggerated the longer it is ignored.

One of our clients (now in her sixties) had been suffering from a recurring nightmare since she was a child. By working on her dream with the help of our telephone service, she was finally able to understand its message. It was reflecting the helplessness that she had felt as a child when she'd had no power to protest. Within the safety and anonymity of the dream-catching call she came to understand what had caused her dream and was able to talk about her childhood experiences for the first time. She had needed to talk to someone who had no connection with her life, and catching her dream enabled her to lay the ghosts to rest. Recurring dreams go away only when the unfinished business they are representing has been resolved.

IS IT NORMAL TO HAVE NIGHTMARES AS AN ADULT?

It is estimated that one million people a week in the UK suffer nightmares. They tend to surface during periods of stress or emotional turmoil or after traumatic events. Nightmares, in fact, help to process difficult feelings and experiences. Dream Catchers believes that there is no such thing as a "bad" dream. Although the experience of a nightmare is obviously distressing, it offers an insight to the things that are troubling you, as well as showing possible ways through your dilemmas. When properly worked through, a nightmare is never as bad as it seems. Some people are left feeling puzzled or guilty about the things they do in their dreams, as they can't conceive of behaving in such ways during waking life. On unravelling their dream, they usually discover that its meaning is not as bad as they feared. Interestingly, nightmares are rare among those who regularly pay attention to their dreams.

WHAT CAN I DO ABOUT MY CHILDREN'S NIGHTMARES?

Children are highly sensitive to change, particularly if it affects the family environment or their school life. In some cases, painful transitions can lead to powerful dreams or nightmares. Helping children to catch their dreams can do much to allay their fears, and they often take to it more easily than adults. Children's dreams can give them a platform from which to express feelings and concerns they might find difficult to articulate in words. Dream-catching can help children to feel less afraid of their nightmares. It can also empower them by offering the chance to create a happy ending for a nightmare that may have been cut short by fear. See Chapter 8 for more information about working with children's dreams.

WHY CAN I GO FOR AGES WITHOUT REMEMBERING A DREAM, AND THEN HAVE SEVERAL POWERFUL DREAMS ALL AT ONCE?

Periods of intense dream activity usually coincide with periods of change in your life. Pregnant women, for example, often experience unusually vivid dreams, and a significant increase in dreaming has been recorded among recent divorcees and those experiencing redundancy and illness. This research confirms the close link between dreams and emotions. Looking at your dreams during troubled periods can help to clarify your options and give you the courage to pursue the best way forward.

Dreams and creativity

Scientific evidence shows that we use very little of our brain's capacity; in fact, some researchers estimate that we use a mere 20 per cent. It is equally clear that a great deal of creativity has been inspired by dreams, so tapping into dreams is obviously a way to get more out of our little grey cells. "Sleep on it" is an injunction we've all heard. Relaxed, as we are when sleeping, we become open to different ways of thinking, are less blinkered and can look at things from different angles. The sleeping mind sorts and processes the many various experiences and dilemmas of daily life in dreams, and tries to find solutions. Whether your problem is practical or creative, focusing your mind on it before you sleep may help you to find an answer in your dreams. Albert Szent-Gyorgi (1893-1986), the Nobel Prize-winning physiologist whose work benefited greatly from his dreams, said: "My work is not finished when I leave my workbench in the afternoon. I go on thinking about my problems all the time and my brain must continue to think about them when I sleep because I wake up… with answers to questions that have been puzzling me."

The following inventions and discoveries illustrate just how effective such dream incubation can be.

BENZENE
The nineteenth-century German chemist Friedrich Kekulé (1829-1896) made a discovery that revolutionized the understanding of organic chemistry. He had been struggling for some time with the chemical structure of carbon atoms when he had the following dream that revealed the ring structure of benzene: "Again the atoms were juggling before my eyes… my mind's eye, sharpened by repeated sights of a similar kind, could now distinguish larger structures of different forms and in long chains, many of them close together; everything was moving in a snake-like and twisting manner. Suddenly… one of the snakes got hold of its own tail and the whole structure was mockingly twisting in front of my eyes. As if struck by lightning, I awoke… Let us learn to dream, gentlemen, and then we may perhaps find the truth."

THE SEWING-MACHINE
We even have dreams to thank for our mass-produced clothes. Elias Howe (1819-1867), the inventor of the modern sewing-machine, was desperate to design a needle that would catch the bobbin thread effectively. For a long time the solution evaded him, but then he had a dream in which he was being attacked by natives with spears which had a hole at the pointed end. The image of the holed spears stayed in his mind and he applied it to his problem. By moving the hole in the needle to the pointed end, he was able to design the first successful sewing-machine.

LIGHT, SOUND AND ACTION

Thomas Edison (1847–1931) is well known as one of history's most successful inventors. He registered over 1000 patents, including those for the electric light bulb, the record-player and the movie camera to name but a few. What is less well known is that he used dreams extensively in the process of invention. He once said, "Ideas come from space." When having difficulty, he would lie down on the bed he kept in his workshop and concentrate his mind on the problem of the moment. He then dozed off, often waking with a new perspective that offered him a creative solution.

PHILOSOPHY

René Descartes (1596–1650), often called the father of modern philosophy, claimed "I think, therefore I am" after pondering his experience with dreams. How was it possible to be certain whether he was awake or dreaming? Eventually he realized that if he was thinking, then he must exist. The impact that his work had on subsequent branches of human thought was enormous.

MUSIC

Former Beatle Sir Paul McCartney (b. 1942) is said to have gone into the recording studio one morning, haunted by a beautiful melody. He asked the other Beatles who had written it, but none of them recognized it. Puzzled as to where he might have heard it, he concluded that it must have been during a dream the previous night. He worked on the tune and it finally emerged as "Yesterday", which went on to become the most recorded song ever.

Dreams have also made a large contribution to the world of classical music. Handel's *Messiah*, many of Richard Wagner's compositions and the Christmas carol "Silent Night" were all inspired by dreams.

LITERATURE

Many works of literature have been dream-inspired. Among them are *The Pilgrim's Progress* (1678–84) by John Bunyan and *Piers Plowman* by William Langland (c. 1330–86). The bizarre, dream-like quality of *Alice's Adventures in Wonderland* (1865) originated in the vivid and surreal dreams that Lewis Carroll had when feverishly ill, while Mary Shelley got the idea for *Frankenstein* (1818) after dreaming that the baby she had recently lost was brought back to life.

Robert Louis Stevenson claimed to receive inspiration for his writings from "dream helpers", who provided him with "better tales than I could fashion myself". Describing how he came to write *The Strange Case of Dr Jekyll and Mr Hyde* (1886), he said: "I can but give an instance or so of what part is done sleeping and what part awake… I had long been trying to write a story on this subject. For two days I went about wracking my brains for a plot of any sort, and on the second night I dreamed the scene at the window and a scene afterward split in two, in which Hyde, pursued for some crime, took the powder and underwent the change in the presence of his pursuers. All the rest was made awake, and consciously."

Human creativity is boundless, but not all of us can rely on our dreams to make world-shattering discoveries or create masterpieces. A dream can work only within the experience and with the raw material of the dreamer. And yet perhaps there is more to it than this. Dreams do seem able to bridge the gap between the known and the unknown, perhaps drawing upon the brain's untapped capacity for wisdom, creativity and invention. During dream-catching we frequently witness ordinary people coping creatively with the dilemmas in their lives by accessing the inner wisdom presented to them in their dreams. If, by reading this book, you are inspired to dream up a new invention, philosophy or work of art, do let us know. ☆

WORKING WITH
YOUR DREAMS

"In our sleep, when the outer world
vanishes, our innermost secret can speak to us
and guide us on this most difficult journey...
Dreams are like mirrors in which we see ourselves.
They reflect back our hidden self, revealing the
true face of our own nature.
In our sleep we are shown the mysteries, the beauty and the
horror of our inner world. Through dreams we can get to
know this strange and yet familiar land. And when we wake,
our dreams can be a doorway through which we can
walk back into this inner world...
into the landscape of the soul."

LLEWELLYN VAUGHN-LEE (1998)

Perhaps the most important aspect of dream-work for you to take on board is that dreams are your own creations; they are what you have made out of your own resources. Every part of a dream has your stamp on it – even the parts you might not wish to own.

Every dreamer weaves a play, which will illuminate the important wishes, conflicts and dilemmas of their waking life. The apparent meaning of a dream will often cover a deeper, richer vein of truth. When characters and objects in a dream are explored and worked with, hidden strengths, insights and new perspectives may be revealed. Old dilemmas and habitual sticking points in your life may be reflected in a dream, providing you with opportunities to find a different perspective on them or a new way through.

Multiple layers; multiple meanings

Sufism is a branch of Islam that teaches the mystical way to spiritual perfection. It believes in conscious evolution and the limitless perfectibility of man. As author Robert Graves wrote: "…the natural Sufi may be as common in the West as in the East, and may come dressed as a general, a merchant, a lawyer, a schoolmaster, a housewife, anything. 'To be in the world but not of it', free from ambition, greed, intellectual pride, blind obedience to custom or awe of persons higher in rank: that is the Sufi's ideal."

The Sufis say that every Sufi story has at least twelve different levels of meaning. Upon the first reading, the reader will enjoy the surprising twist to the story – after some time and several readings new perspectives will emerge. Although the first meaning remains, it will seem but a first draft of a much more elaborate creation. And so it is with the many layers and reflections within dreams.

To catch a dream

Freud called dreams the "royal road to the unconscious". He believed that if dreamers were to access the full meaning of their dreams, it would show them their lifetime's task. For most of us who have set out on a path of self-discovery, identifying the task is half the battle won. Over the coming pages you will be able to take the first basic steps to catching and working with your own dreams.

Working with dreams
- Work only on your own dreams, never someone else's, unless you are working together.
- Be willing to look deeply into the dream and interact with its different characters and objects.
- Set aside your preconceptions.
- Be prepared to look at things from a different perspective.

STEP 1 – UNWRAPPING THE DREAM

The most effective way to explore the layers of a dream is to retell it or write it down in as much detail as possible, as if it is happening in the present. Make sure you include your accompanying responses. Notice your feelings (joy, distaste, fear, curiosity) and also your bodily responses (trembling, tension, warmth, cold). Try to let the dream story flow without censoring it. If you notice yourself making changes, pay attention to what those changes are and why you are making them. Know that this story is for you. You don't have to tell it to anyone else, although exploring your dream with another dream-worker will nearly always enable you to see more of what the dream is presenting to you. For example:

"I am driving in a sports car, hurtling along a narrow, winding country lane. The top is down and I can feel a sharp breeze in my hair. I am not particularly comfortable. I am cold and feel a bit cramped. The car is going too fast. I feel excited, more apprehensive than excited. I fear that I am going to crash."

Note the fine details of your dream, its colours, textures, sounds and smells.
"The car is new, black and shiny. The lane is very green with tall hedges and I can't see anything but the road ahead of me. It seems to be early morning, a bit misty, and the road is wet. It smells of greenery. I can hear only the wind in my ears."

Notice how you were feeling during your dream.
"I am not comfortable. I'm cold, cramped and anxious."

And when you woke up?
"I awoke with a start and it took me a little time to calm myself down."

41

How are you feeling now, while reliving the story?
"Right now I am wondering how I got into this position, and it feels kind of familiar."
(You can explore later how you did get into this position.)

Let yourself be open to what you are experiencing.
"I'd rather not know about this, yet I know it's important for me in my life right now."

Notice any feelings that surface. Just let them be there.
"I feel a bit shaky and a little tearful." [Swallows nervously and clasps hands tightly]

Don't rush over any discomfort. The tone of a dream story contains the key to unravelling its meaning for you.
"I think I've been building up to this for some time. I've not been feeling well for a while. But I'm not actually sure what the dream's about."

You can see from this example that a dream does not necessarily have to be long or dramatic to be important.

STEP 2 – TURNING THE PIECES OVER
This part of the work is a little like starting a jigsaw. It's usual to turn all the pieces face up and then start the sorting process, but everybody has his or her own method. Some people sort the edges and start to build from the corners, while others go for colours or shapes. You need to find your own approach and begin to recognize the pieces and shapes of your dream. Eventually you will see how they fit together. Starting with something that excites your interest will quickly take you to the core of your dream, but it doesn't really matter where you start, as the important theme of the dream will be reflected throughout its unfolding.

Choose an element of the dream that seems particularly interesting to you and then explore it. Perhaps your curiosity is aroused by a peculiar object, or you may have a sense of well-being, sadness or longing when you recall a certain scene.
"The racing car intrigues me because I enjoy speed."

Imagine that you are that object and describe yourself in the dream in the present tense. Take your time, close your eyes and visualize the object. Then picture yourself as the object and start describing yourself. For example:

"I am a fast black sports car, with sleek lines and fat tyres. I am hurtling down a winding road with my wheels squealing at every turn. I feel as if I am out of control and on the verge of crashing. I wish my driver would put the brakes on."

Describing parts of the dream in this spontaneous way will enable you to make sense of your dream symbols, and their significance will become more apparent. Through using this form of description you will start to make connections with the words you are saying more easily than if you described the car as an object being observed from a distance. The idea is to bypass the part of you that objectifies and intellectualizes. Logic does have a part in dream-work, but during this turning-over and recognizing process, you need to trust your first thoughts, feelings and associations no matter how unexpected or strange they may seem. Even focusing on one simple image can produce useful insights.

A woman came to a Dream Catchers workshop with just a single image that puzzled her. At the time of her dream she was facing some changes in her relationship and wondering whether to make the commitment of living with her partner.

"I had this dream of a red octopus, a bright red octopus, and I really can't make head or tail of it."

Imagine that you are the octopus. Describe yourself.
"Well, I'm big and I'm very, very red. That's all. I'm very red."

Tell me, Octopus, how come you are so red?
[Exclaims suddenly] *"I'm red with effort, with all the effort I am putting into this relationship. Oh, that is so true!* [Laughs delightedly] *I didn't realize it, but I'm working so hard. I need to ease off."*

This dreamer managed to get to the crux of the dream's message so quickly by allowing herself to voice her instinctive, unthinking response to the question. Learn to speak your first thoughts so that you can capture the small voice in the back of your mind before your more rational, conscious mind takes over and replies "in character". This inner voice speaks from your uncensored feelings and can provide you with a vital link to your dream messages.

If your first associations with an image seem to get nowhere, you can step down one level and imagine that you are explaining the elements and symbols of the dream to a Martian who needs things spelt out very simply. In the car dream, for example:

"I am a car, a vehicle that transports people from place to place."

Still don't get any feeling or sense of it? Then go to the next basic level of description – the material qualities of the car.

"A car is a container made out of metal. I am hard and protective because I can travel at speed and I carry people around in me who need protection from the elements and the possibility of accidents."

How are you like this car? Do you feel as though you are constantly transporting people from place to place? Are you hard and protective? Do you feel as if your life is travelling at speed? Even if you can make no immediate connection, don't be discouraged. Keep turning the pieces over, just as you would with a jigsaw. Sometimes the piece that is left over, the one that doesn't fit, is simply not being held in the proper perspective; eventually its place will become clear.

If working with an image seems to yield nothing, just move on to another aspect of your dream. Remember that each part of the dream is functioning for the resolution of the whole; there will be echoes and reflections of the main message throughout the dream. If not this piece, then another will give you an essential clue.

STEP 3 – MAKING SENSE OF THE DREAM (THE "AH-HA" FACTOR)

You might already have made some connections for yourself by describing your dream as if it was happening at the present moment. Often the words and phrases you use will have a familiar or resonant ring to them. When you hear yourself saying them, you might feel as if something has just slotted into place. You could make a note of these associations that seem to ring a bell. Then, when you have finished turning over the pieces of the dream, go back and reflect on them. You might be surprised at how they relate to each other and how accurately they reflect who you are and any concerns that you have at the time.

When you make a particularly significant connection, you might feel a sudden sense of exhilaration, or even a physical sensation, like a bolt out of the blue. This is the "ah-ha" factor: a profound recognition of something you know to be correct. If you reach this point, it is a good idea to note down your response and spend some time thinking about how it relates to your life. There may be steps you could take to remedy or positively influence a situation. Sit for a while with the new perspectives your insights have offered you. After a while, you will become clearer about what, if any, action you should take. Know that whether your dream's message is affirmative or a warning, it now gives you an opportunity to influence your circumstances positively.

Look at the words and phrases you use when exploring your dream. Do they sound familiar? Perhaps you have heard them in a particular context or spoken by a particular person? Pay attention and don't rush over these associations. If a phrase has jumped out at you, it usually has some significance.

"I do hurtle around. My wife says I hurtle. I am being driven at speed… yes… sometimes I feel I am being driven too hard and too fast."

So you are a fast, sleek, fat-tyred car. How do you make sense of that? Ask yourself how you are like this car now in your life.

"Well… I do like to look good. I work out regularly and like to be noticed."

How are you fast? Free-associate with this concept of being fast, discover what it means for you and how speeding in the dream context could apply to your life at present. Do you feel that you are being carried away by something? Do you need to put the brakes on part of your life? Only you know the answers to these questions and what they relate to.

"Well, the job is a bit high-pressured, and in the morning I seem to hit the floor running."

Are you sleek? What is sleek? Smooth, shapely, aerodynamic? Polished and streamlined? Use your own words. Have fun, play.

"As I said, that's how I like to be, but it takes a lot of energy keeping myself so highly polished."

Identify with your dream situation and its symbols. Remember that each part of the dream is playing a role for you. Trust your first thoughts and associations. What part of you is like the fat tyres? Your first association may be with spare tyres round your middle. Does this association fit with the sleek image? Only you know if it relates to your fat spare tyre.

"What fat spare tyre? I don't have one of those. No, my association is with smooth, quiet, whispering, solid motoring. I'm a smooth operator and usually I've got a good solid set of wheels under me. But in this dream they are being made to squeal because of the reckless way I'm being driven. Ah-ha...I get it!"

Be careful not to jump to conclusions too quickly. Make a note of any connections (and resistances) and keep exploring. You can always come back to something later. If you can find no more associations and feel stuck, it might be necessary to get down to the fundamental materials of the object, their physical properties and characteristics. Persist, go in deeper. You can look at a particular part of the image more closely. Describe to the Martian what tyres really are. For example:

"I am made of rubber, the same stuff as balls are made of. I bounce, but I can become shredded if I'm driven badly."

What is rubber?
"I am made of a material that is strong and flexible, able to grip as well as bounce. I can provide a buffer from knocks or a rocky road."

Now we're getting somewhere! How are you like these rubber tyres?
"Well, I'm a pretty flexible sort of chap."

How do these tyres relate to your present situation?
"I don't think my tyres are in very good shape at present. I feel a bit flat, not quite up to the mark. I've not been looked after or driven very well."

Already this dreamer, through expanding just one of the dream's images, is discovering more about how it relates to him. If you still can't make sense of this for yourself, be the wheels. What are wheels?
"I am round and smooth. I shift large weights smoothly. I am turned by an engine or pushed by some outside force. I don't have any momentum

of my own unless I am pushed, pulled or rolled down a sharp incline."

How are you like this?
"I suppose I am feeling a bit as if I am not in charge of my own destiny at the moment. Mortgage, bills, new family and so forth."

STEP 4 – WORKING WITH THE PEOPLE IN A DREAM

Working with characters in a dream can offer particularly useful insights, especially if the characters are playing a significant part in the dream. Put yourself in their position; give them a voice; imagine what they would say to you within the dream; try to get right into their character, even if they seem threatening. Be aware that they are in your dream representing a part of you. Even if you know them well in real life, describe them out loud or on paper as if to someone who has never met them.

Use the same method of exploration with a person as you do with an object, even if it's someone you know in real life. Try to speak with their voice and personality as you see it. Trust your responses as you work through these following questions:

- What do you look like?
- What's important for you (as the character) in the dream?
- How are you reacting?
- What are you doing?
- What happens in the dream (as seen through their eyes)?
- What would they want to say?

Perhaps they are saying something in the dream, or they would like to say something. Perhaps they are driving the car? Let them speak. For example:
"I am so and so driving a very fast car. I am too big for the car and rather squashed into the seat. However, I am enjoying the ride... or was enjoying the ride until I realized that I can't use the brakes effectively and I seem to be hurtling out of control."

How are you (the dreamer) like this? Squashing yourself into the driver's seat of too small a vehicle and enjoying the ride until you realize that you are going too fast and can't access the brakes? Does this make any sense to you? Does it relate to a relationship perhaps? A career move? You, the dreamer, must make the connection.

STEP 5 – DREAM CONVERSATIONS

"The dream is a conversation between humanity and God," said the Prophet Muhammad. Indeed, dreams can be seen as internal conversations bringing unconscious impulses, feelings, wisdoms and insights to consciousness. You can find out more about yourself through any dream situation by having a conversation between different parts of your dream, such as between the driver and the car. Be spontaneous – as if ad libbing a script. For example, what does the car say?

"Put your foot on the brake!"

[As driver] *"I can't get at the right angle... there's not enough room. I feel faint..."*

"At least take your foot off the accelerator."

[As driver] *"Not enough room to do that either."*

"Well, use the gears to slow down."

[As driver] *"That I can do."*

What does this exchange suggest? Perhaps you should find out how you could currently "downshift" your life to take things more slowly. Are you unable to take direct action? Is there too little room for manoeuvre?

STEP 6 – CONVERSING WITH THE DREAM ITSELF

After engaging fully with the dream-catching process and working through the dream, you could now ask the dream itself what its message is. It is important to continue the same instinctive, imaginative way of responding that you used when associating with the different elements of the dream (Steps 2 and 3). Often the message will come through simply and to the point. For example, "My message to you is take more care of yourself. Give yourself more time and space to breathe. Speed needs to be supported by an effective braking system."

Ask an object in the dream what its purpose is, generally and/or specifically. Trust the first response; it might surprise you. Remember the red octopus in Step 2 who said, "I'm red with all the effort I am putting into this relationship."

Are you getting the idea? Often a dreamer needs to work only part of a dream thoroughly in order to uncover its message. Unwrapping the other parts will, of course, be useful, especially if the message still seems unclear.

However, further working will nearly always show the same dilemma from a different perspective.

STEP 7 – WORKING AROUND THE DREAM

The dream provides a basis for exploration. You do not have to be limited by the dream's boundaries. If the dream is unfinished or interrupted, you can continue to explore its images and relationships in waking fantasy (see page 58). Often a dream will stop in mid-air because we have been woken. Sometimes we stop the dream ourselves because it feels too scary or we don't really want to know its outcome. Freud had a lot to say about self-censorship of dreams (see Chapter 2). However, for whatever the reason the dream has been cut, we can pick up the script in waking life – and here the support of another dream-catcher is useful. Having another person to work with helps us to go into unknown or frightening territory.

Sometimes what led up to the dream is important. A dream-catcher might have asked the person dreaming of the car, "What happened just before you got into the car?" Or "How come you squeezed yourself into this car?"

"I was trying to impress a friend/my boss/a girl."

"So, trying to impress got you into this dilemma… how does that fit with you in real life?"

You do not have to stay with the dream just as it appeared to you. You are working with your imaginative process, which is closely linked to the dreaming process. By letting your imagination run free you might access a more imaginative solution to a dilemma and then be able to utilize it within your life. Remember that there are no boundaries in your dreams, waking fantasies or free-associations – there are no limits to the amount of awareness and inspiration that can be found. If something is possible in a dream, it may also be possible in your life. Your dream is your creation: you have woven it and come up with these images. Many good ideas have come to inventors through their dreaming. That same sort of creativity may also be available to you through your daydreams.

What happens next? You could find out by finishing the dream. Continue the story in the present, as if it's happening now. Trust the images and thoughts that come. What happens next in the car dream?

"Well, I start to shift down. I can just work the clutch and grate the

gears to slow down the car but we are still rolling pretty fast. Wait, I'm going to stall the car and run it up on to the side of the road; there's a grassy bank with a hedge at the top that could act as a natural brake. I need a natural break, too true!"

Often with this type of dream-working you will hear yourself saying something that has a ring of truth to it. You are getting the message. Perhaps something is missing in the dream. Think of that missing thing and imagine where it might be and why it is missing.

"My watch is missing from my wrist. It's a really expensive watch and I'm really proud of it. It was given to me in the last job I had. I feel a bit sad when I remember that. That last job was great, but I left it because it didn't put me in the fast lane soon enough. I wanted to speed up my prospects."

(He is definitely getting the message.)

STEP 8 – IDENTIFY WITH THE MISSING OBJECT
What is a watch?
"I am a timepiece. I regulate the day and help my owner to pace himself."

What happened to you?
"He forgot me... left me on the bathroom shelf this morning. He was in too much of a hurry."

A fuller picture is emerging now and the dreamer cannot help but get the message of his dream. It's now up to him whether he will apply these insights to his life and give himself a natural break.

You could follow this same process with other aspects of the dream, going on to look at the country lane (for example, meandering around, not going anywhere in particular, not built for speed). Or you could be the countryside (open, spacious, fresh, green, natural). How are you like this? Could you benefit if you allowed yourself to be like this? Trust your first responses and associate with your dream images in your own way. It's up to you, the dreamer, to make sense of your own dream.

Dreams can often give access to important information that you have skimmed over, taken for granted, or not evaluated correctly. Within the car example, a decision had been taken based upon wants rather than needs. The driver was not conscious of the personal advantages of his previous job, so did not negotiate a nourishing structure for himself in the new one.

Nightmares

As we have seen, dreams often carry messages about issues that we need to pay attention to. If we are not able to access these messages, or we are not dealing with the situations our dreams are warning us about, they will start to speak louder and louder until they force us to wake up. We work with a nightmare in the same way as an ordinary dream.

GILLIAN'S NIGHTMARE
"I am in a large Roman arena... I seem to be one of the gladiators and there is a capacity crowd. We are pushing gigantic carts before us made out of huge tree trunks with wooden wheels. They are slow to get moving but travel with force and speed once in action, although difficult to steer. Sprinting behind this vehicle, I am horrified to see that we are heading for a group of people cowering against the high walls of the arena. They seem powerless to escape and are facing certain death from the sharp points of the tree trunks. I recognize two friends among them and wake shocked and trembling before the impact."

Gillian worked on this dream, first describing herself as the amphitheatre.
"I am a large arena built for the entertainment of Roman emperors and the Roman populace. I am filled with slaves, some of whom are gladiators."

What is a gladiator?
"I am a fighter, strong and desperate to stay alive. I have risen from the slave ranks by virtue of my strength, prowess and cunning. I will stay strong and alive no matter what. I can have no thought for the others whom I have to annihilate in order to survive."

How are you like that?
Gillian recognized that she was a fighter, a survivor – unwilling to show that she

51

was vulnerable and relentless in her belief that to survive she had to be strong no matter what. She was quite oblivious to the fact that others felt wiped out by her.

Be the victims.
"We are thrown into this arena by people who are stronger and bigger than us. The gladiators, who are also victims of this system, must try to kill us. We bear them no malice, but will try to escape from their crushing implements in the best way we can. We are defenceless, except for the companionship and support we have for each other, so we hug and care for each other and try as best we can to protect the young and defenceless."

How are you like that?
"Not at all! I'm a fighter…I'll fight to the death. I won't just stand there hugging and weeping and be mown down. To fight and die is better than to hug and die. At least that way I won't feel so powerless."

Be one of the huge carts.
"I am a massive instrument of death — difficult to get moving but hard to stop once I'm under way. I'm made of natural materials of primitive design, but I am being used for an unnatural purpose."

What would be a natural purpose?
"I could be used to build a shelter rather than annihilate a victim."
(Bells are starting to ring.)

How are you like that?
"I'm using my natural self unnaturally, to annihilate rather than shelter my friends."

Speak to your friends.
"For God's sake, get out of the way! I can't control this cart and it's going to kill you."
"Stop pushing it, then."
"Even if I stop, you are going to die anyway as others will take you away. Uh, oh — you are going to die anyway…"
Tears fall as she makes a connection: she realizes that two of her friends, who

have not met each other, are about to leave England for foreign lands. *"They are going to die to me anyway no matter what I do."*

At this point she recognized that she had cut off from her friends since they had told her they were leaving (a natural but primitive reaction to hurt). Her dream told her that there was something else she could do.

The next day she rang her friends and arranged to meet. At the meetings she told them how she felt about their leaving. Yes, she was angry; in fact, anger had helped her deal with the hurt and loss she felt, but more than this, she could now embrace them, tell them how much she loved them and how important they were to her.

We need to recognize and acknowledge our own reflection in the monsters of our dreams. Then they will lose their power to make us afraid. In Jungian terms, this is called facing the shadow.

The shadow

Carl Jung (1875-1961) wrote of the shadow, the dark side of the personality: "The shadow cast by the conscious mind of the individual contains the hidden, repressed and unfavourable aspects of the personality."

He pointed out that this darkness is not simply the opposite of good aspects of our personality. The shadow also has positive qualities – normal instincts and creative impulses.

Jung also said, "Through dreams one becomes acquainted with aspects of one's own personality that for various reasons one has preferred not to look at too closely." This is what he called the "realization of the shadow". (He used the term "shadow" for this unconscious part of the personality because in dreams it often appears in the form of a dark or threatening person.) The shadow represents unknown or little-known attributes and qualities of the ego. It is not the whole of the unconscious personality.

Just to be good is not enough. Choosing to allow only the "light and shining" aspects of ourselves can make us blind to the benefits of withdrawal and retreat. If good (sweet and light) people do not learn to use the positive attributes of the dark that are essential for self-protection, they could leave themselves open to exploitation and/or exhaustion.

When we first become aware that our inner intentions are more than we consciously show, we may feel disquieted and ashamed. As a result, it is common to resist identifying with unpleasant or uncomfortable parts of our dreams. It is difficult to own those impulses and characteristics (aggression, pride, selfishness, fear, vulnerability) in ourselves that we condemn in others. The shadow usually exhibits feelings and behaviours in a way that makes it difficult to own and integrate them into our lives. "Whether a shadow becomes our friend or enemy depends largely upon ourselves. The shadow becomes hostile only when it is ignored or misunderstood. Whatever form it takes, the function of the shadow is to represent the opposite side of ourselves and embody just those qualities we most dislike in other people."

Jung believed that the shadow often contained valuable and vital forces that ought to be assimilated into actual experience rather than repressed. "Somewhere, right at the bottom of one's own being, one generally knows where one should go and what one should do... There are times when the clown we call 'I' behaves in such a distracting fashion that the inner voice cannot make its presence felt."

There is a significant difference between dream-catching and Jungian dream analysis. In dream-catching we do not believe that another person can effectively work out what our dream symbols mean. An intellectual dream-working process can, by Jung's own admission, be hit or miss. A dream-catcher will always ask a dreamer to freely associate with all the symbols and people within their dream. Owning and acting out these various parts will throw light on the shadow and enable the dreamer to allow the true note of long-suppressed feeling to be heard. (For more illustrations of dream-catching nightmares see Chapter 8.)

Waking dreams

Also known as guided fantasies, waking dreams can be worked with in exactly the same way as ordinary dreams. The basic outline of a fantasy is told and the dreamer fills it out and colours in their own experience. They are then shown how to use the dream-catcher's process to unravel the message in their waking dream.

Each time we take a group through a guided fantasy, we are impressed by how many variations of the "journey" are possible. Waking dreams illustrate how dreams and fantasies are representative of the individual dreamer. Just as in a dream, each participant will weave their own tapestry, imbued with the colours and textures of their inner world.

PREPARING FOR A WAKING FANTASY

Settle yourself comfortably with your back supported and your feet on the floor. Close your eyes. Take three full breaths and as you let them go, drop your shoulders and let yourself relax. Drop your muscles so that you are supported just by your spinal column on the chair. Now let your breathing happen naturally, and with each exhaled breath, let your self "drop" a little further.

As you are sitting, thoughts will enter your mind and you may be distracted. Just let these thoughts go with the next out breath and allow your in breath to follow easily. The aim is to "drop down inside" as you breathe out, exhaling any thoughts and distractions. As you inhale, allow your breath to fill up the space inside before you also let it drop out. If you practise this way, you may come to notice that you no longer have the sensation of dropping down with your out breath. You may come to a stop, a quiet place. Let yourself rest there, breathing easily in and out.

As you go through the waking dream that follows, allow yourself to free-associate. Trust the first images that come to you, even if they don't suit your idea of how you would want them to be. These images are straight from your id (the instinctive part of your unconscious) and have the same import and potency as dream symbols. If you want to change them, notice how and why you do so. Remember that your spontaneous responses will yield the most productive insights. Allow your waking dream to progress at its own pace, even if you fall a bit behind the commentary. Note how you feel throughout it.

Give yourself plenty of time for each question. Try to feel as if you are really experiencing the things described.

THE WAKING FANTASY BEGINS

Imagine that you are on a journey. Let images drop into your mind as you listen. Don't struggle with them. Picture them in detail as you move along on your journey.
- How are you travelling?
- What can you see as you travel?
- What are your surroundings?
- Are you alone or accompanied?

CHAPTER 4

- Who is with you?
- How do you feel as you travel?
- How comfortable are you?
- What are you wearing?
- Do you have much luggage?

Suddenly your journey is interrupted.
- What has caused this interruption?
- What can you do?
- What do you do about it?
- How does the wait make you feel?
- Where are you when this happens?

Now you are able to continue your journey.
- What has happened to allow this?

You meet someone on this journey.
- Do you know him/her?

He/she is going to travel alongside you.
- How do you feel about this?
- How are you together (comfortable, happy, awkward, etc.)?

Now your companion is going to leave you.
- How do you feel about this?

Continue on your way without him/her.
- How is the journey different for you now?

Soon you will see your destination in the distance.
- What do you notice about it?
- What can you see?
- As you approach it, how do you feel?

You are now nearing the end of your journey.
- What do you notice?

Now you have arrived.
- How do you feel?
- What do you do?

Night is starting to fall and you need to make your way to a safe place.
- How do you find this?
- Where is this place?

Settle down for the night and rest. After resting for a while, allow your eyes to open and let yourself return to the present.

Write down or tell someone about your journey in the present, as if it is happening now. You can work with your journey in the same way as you would with a dream. When you have finished, read through the following examples of waking dreams from a Dream Catchers workshop. (It's better to read them after rather than before working through your waking dream.)

WAKING DREAM EXAMPLE 1 – RED DRESS AND BICYCLE
"I am cycling along a track wearing a beautifully flowing red dress. It's a lovely day and I feel very happy, but the dress keeps getting caught in the chain and eventually rips. I have to stop and untangle it."

Be the bicycle.
"I am a strong and sturdy machine that can get you from place to place quickly and efficiently. I am eco-friendly."
(Laughter as the group recognizes her style and that she had indeed cycled across London for this workshop.)

Be the red dress.
"Oh! I am soft and flowing, billowing out as Jane cycles along. I am made of fine material. I am ever so expensive and pretty."
(She is tearful as she recognizes a well-hidden part of herself; she is actually dressed in dark trousers and top.)

Say that again.
"I am made of fine material and I'm ever so expensive and pretty.

[As herself] *I never think of myself in this way."*

Do so now. How do you feel being so fine and expensive and pretty?
"It's lovely!"

You are lovely! Now, take the risk. Imagine that you are the red dress and move about the room as if you were made of this fine flowing material.
(She does so, at first hesitantly, then with greater confidence, until she is swirling and swooping joyfully.)

How are you doing?
"Oh, I am lovely!" [Laughter and appreciation from the group] *"I never let myself do this.* [Quietly] *It was my sister who was the pretty one."*

WAKING DREAM EXAMPLE 2 – PRISON OR SANCTUARY?

"I am walking in the Rockies. There is no one around and I am walking along a deserted highway. There is a track off to the left, going up into the hills, and I follow that but I'm feeling very anxious that no one uses it and if I were to get lost or hurt, I wouldn't be found. The track is well beaten, however, and as I make my way up, I enjoy the view and the silence. When it comes to finding a place to rest, I go into a cave and lie down."
(This daydreamer was not happy with her journey and felt that she should have kept to the highway.)

Be the path.
"I am a path, narrow, difficult and winding, and I lead up the hill. I am well used, even though there is nobody but Sarah on me at present."

Can you identify with being like this?
"Oh, yes. Well used, difficult and winding!"

Be the cave.
"Oh, I don't like this cave either. There's nothing here: it's so bare – just walls. It's so boring. Perhaps I could put something in it, or on the walls?"

You could, but be the cave first and see what comes from that.
"OK. I am a cave, a dark and silent hole... I don't like this..."

Keep being the cave.
"I am hollowed out from the hillside and I provide shelter for animals and people from storms and the dangers of darkness at night."

What are you like inside?
"Well, inside I am really dark and quiet." [Pauses and becomes thoughtful]

How is this for you, to be dark and quiet?
"I'm surprised. It's really nice, sort of peaceful, not like the busy highway with its hustle and bustle and traffic."

You had thought that perhaps you could put some things into the cave and on the walls. What does the cave feel about that?
"Oh, no! Don't do that...you would spoil me. Just rest in me..." [Silence and tears] *"I didn't know I had this space inside me. I have always been so frightened of being quiet and in the dark, yet it's lovely. I feel so peaceful and rested."*

Well, you can go there any time. This space is in you – it's yours.

Sarah was a recovering addict, and her difficult life of addiction and pain was reflected in this waking dream by the busy traffic on the highway and the much-used path up the hill. She had the courage to persist with the working through, even though her first response was to dislike and dismiss the images that came to her.

Sarah's experience provides a wonderful example of working with the "fertile void", a place of frightening nothingness that when explored and rested in becomes something fertile and nourishing. (A similar concept is found in Sufism, which says that the usefulness of a jug is the space inside.) ☆

Catch your dream

Here is a resumé of the steps involved in the dream-catching process.

1 Unwrapping the dream
- Write down or tell your dream as if it's happening now in the present.
- Note any sensations, feelings or associations you might have had during the dreaming or in the retelling.

2 Turning the pieces over
- Choose a part of the dream that has the most emotional content or attracts your interest.
- Be that part and describe the dream from its perspective.
- Pay attention to what this part needs, wants or is saying. Pay particular attention to any key words or phrases that reverberate for you.
- Identify with all the aspects of your dream in this way and then ask yourself, "How am I like this?"

3 Making sense of the dream
- Ask yourself what this dream-play has to do with your life at present.
- Note down any familiar symbols and their previous significance.
- Pay particular attention to any phrase or description that strikes a chord in you.

4 Working with people in the dream
- Describe the person in detail and identify with his/her role in the dream.

5 Dream conversations
- Have a dialogue between different aspects of the dream. For example, in Sarah's dream you could imagine what the path and the road might say to each other.

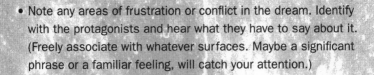

• Note any areas of frustration or conflict in the dream. Identify with the protagonists and hear what they have to say about it. (Freely associate with whatever surfaces. Maybe a significant phrase or a familiar feeling, will catch your attention.)

6 Conversing with the dream
• Ask the dream and the dream's characters what their message is.
• Ask an object what its purpose is.

7 Working around the dream
• Imagine what happened before the dream and imagine what happens next.
• Notice if anything is missing from the dream. Identify with it and explore its "off-stage" situation.

8 Working with nightmares
• Remember that a nightmare is never as bad as it seems. The frightening part of the dream is nearly always representative of something in yourself or your life that is shouting because it needs attention.
• Identify with each aspect of the nightmare as if it were an ordinary dream.
• Give the shadow aspect a voice. You might be surprised at what it says to you. Once faced, it will fade.

5

ACTIONING
DREAM MESSAGES

CHAPTER 5

During times of transition and trial, dreams are often more active than usual. Research has shown, for example, that people dream more during marital break-ups, probably because they need to come to terms with all the emotions that the situation provokes. Unexpressed feelings need an outlet. The evidence that sleeping subjects prevented from dreaming become more nervous, exhausted, bad-tempered and generally debilitated than those left to dream suggests that dreams are essential to well-being.

Whether dreams are remembered or not, they do the work of sorting and releasing tension every night of our lives. Even if the dreams are never worked with, they continue to fulfil that purpose. By connecting with our dreams and actioning their messages, however, we can become active rather than passive participants in the evolution of our consciousness. Why sit in the dark when you can strike a match?

New possibilities

Sometimes dreams are quite explicit about offering us a new opportunity or perspective. At other times, the message may be more cryptic. Helen has an example of this.

"The evening before I was to be interviewed at an institute where I wished to study, I asked for a dream. I woke early the next morning without recalling one. Seeing that it was only 6 a.m., I decided there was time enough to catch one, so I turned over and put myself back to sleep with a request for a dream. I awoke at 7.30 with no dream, just the image of an uncooked loaf of bread. I felt disappointed, but decided to work with this single image in waking fantasy."

As the loaf of bread.
"I am a soft, round cottage loaf, all ready to go into the oven and be nicely cooked."

What was missing?
"The oven."

So be the oven that this loaf is wanting to be cooked in.

"I am a heavy, cast-iron oven with a big clanking door and I cook only square loaves of bread."

Somewhat stunned, Helen said:
"But I like being a round loaf. I could make myself square because I am still soft and pliant, but I don't want to be square and I'm not going to change my shape for you."

Helen faced a dilemma: she was about to present herself, a round loaf, to an institute that she instinctively saw as square. What to do?

Later at the interview she was asked how she felt about entering the training. Without thinking of the consequences, she blurted out her dream. Needless to say, they didn't let her into their oven! They invited her to attend an on-going group for a year and then to reapply. She was devastated and suffered a great blow to her ego. It took a lot of reassurance from friends and colleagues to restore her confidence.

Eventually, Helen did join the training course and the institute assigned her to a group conductor and a supervisor, who, each in their own way, were rebels. She was grateful to them. She retained her cottage shape and become a little less impatient and reactive in the cooking process. She has since made her way in the world as a gestaltist, considerably enriched by the wealth of learning and experience that she accumulated in the process of becoming a group analyst.

It was quite another type of dream that pushed Helen to embark upon her gestalt training.

HELEN'S "TRAINING" DREAM
"I am entering the railway station and a huge American-type train is steaming at the platform. There is a general hustle and bustle as it is preparing to leave and I am not at all sure whether this is my train or not. At another platform, a suburban train is also preparing to leave for London."

At the time, Helen was engaged in a weekend gestalt workshop and had been wondering whether to opt into a longer training process. During the workshop, the facilitator asked Helen where she was in relation to her decision, and she told him she was no further ahead. Then she remembered the dream. When invited to work with it, she was a little reluctant, not quite knowing how it related to her predicament.

Be the train.
"I am a large steam train, old-fashioned, solid and shining, green, racing green. I am at Cambridge railway station and preparing to leave."

Tell us more.
"I don't know any more."

Use your imagination. Where has the train come from and where is it going?
"Well, I am a large train...very large and long. In fact [warming to the task] *I extend way beyond the platform. There are only a few carriages open to new passengers, so they had better be quick because I am about to leave. I am going...around the world! Yes, I travel around the world, stopping for only about ten minutes at each station to get supplies, take on new passengers and let others off. I am an amazing train: each of my carriages has a different feel to it, different culture, different food and lifestyle. My passengers can move around me and experience the cultures of the world. I'm a truly international train and it takes me ten years to do the circuit. If you don't get on me now, I won't be back this way for ten years."*

Is Helen going to get on board?
"I'm not sure." [As Helen] *"Let me talk to the train driver."*

As the train driver.
"OK, I'm the train driver. I am a large American, with a train driver's cap and blue overalls. I've got dirty hands and a sweaty brow. What is it you want to know?"

Tell me about this train.
"Well, it's a mighty fine train."

How long have you been working on it?
"25,000 years." [Silence]

How come you are still just a train driver?
"I do what I like and I like what I do."

And with that, Helen leapt on board.

At a later time, Helen worked with the image of the suburban train also at a platform in the same dream. She discovered that it was a somewhat muted vehicle, steady, chugging and reliable, and realized that it represented her group analytic training. Throughout the next few years she would dream of one or other of these trains, and came to recognize that they symbolized her training opportunities.

These examples illustrate one way dreamers can begin to decipher their dreams. By choosing an image (the train) and expanding it via waking fantasy, using free-association and role play, Helen discovered, albeit with much hesitancy and self-examination, that she did indeed want to begin training.

Making the connections between dreaming and reality

After reading Chapter 4 you might already have some idea of what your dream is talking to you about. How do the feelings, insights and statements that have emerged from your dream-working apply or fit with your life at present? Do they relate to a relationship, a health issue, an inner fear? Simply identifying what part of your life your dream is addressing might be enough for you. You may feel satisfied already and wish to change nothing or take no action.

Your dream could be inviting or challenging you to address your life situation differently. You can ask yourself how your new-found awareness could be put to work for you. Making connections from your dream to everyday issues may have already given you some insight into how you need to change or rearrange your life, and you may need to look a bit further in order to clarify how to action your dream's message. In the train dream, for example, it became clear to Helen that the train was representing her "training" possibilities but she was still not sure whether to embark on it or not. It was only after working further in creative fantasy and hearing the words she had spoken as the train driver – "I like what I do and I do what I like" – that she clearly "felt" the way forward and had no hesitation about clambering on board.

Trying to work things out just by thinking them over can be a frustrating business, often giving no clear answer. Living a dream as it is, or extending the dream story when it is unfinished, brings life to the issue, sometimes providing a physical feeling of certainty about what you need to do.

Working with resistances and blocks

At times, the way out of an indecisive or stuck place is to pay attention to the hesitation or resistance you may have about moving on. No matter how obvious the way forward might seem to another person, you may still need to hesitate. It is important not to push through resistant feelings. Paradoxically, as demonstrated in the following example, the more important the issue, the more resistant you may be to making changes.

JUDITH'S DREAM

A young woman called Judith, who had been away from her home country for some time, was feeling very isolated both socially and culturally. She was at the time working with anorexic adolescents and during a supervision group, when presenting her work with a client who was starving because of her need to control her environment, she recalled a dream she herself had had some years previously.

"I'm walking in a forest and come upon a clearing with a concrete bunker. As I approach the bunker, I notice a listless and emaciated herd of cows. I'm about to get closer to the bunker to investigate the plight of the cows when two vicious dogs chase me away. One of the dogs is red raw without his coat of hair. I run for my life and escape by barricading myself in an outhouse. I am eventually rescued by a woman, who appears evasive and unaware of my ordeal."

When Judith had identified with the cows, she saw that they were starving and longing to be released. The concrete bunker, however, was unmoving and rigid in its duty of containment and protection. As Judith worked with the dream and conversed with the separate parts of it, she came to realize how much like these cows she felt. She had tried to keep free of emotional pain by isolating herself, and now she felt starved of affection and emotional nourishment. She also could identify with the concrete bunker, holding firmly and solidly in a misguided defence of vulnerability. Judith tells the story in her own words:

"I was asked to be the concrete bunker in the dream. To this day I remember saying, 'I'm a concrete bunker. I'm made of stuff that does not crack. I've got cows within me that are starving. Nothing is going in and nothing is coming out.'"

Judith was asked to repeat the above lines a few times, and then asked to be a cow in the bunker.
"I am a domestic animal. I need to be looked after. I can't fend for myself. I'm starving and will die unless I get food and water."
(People new to dream-catching may find this type of identification difficult at first, but we encourage them to do so as the words they use in their description will graphically illustrate their present dilemmas.)

What is your purpose, cow?
"My purpose is to produce calves and milk."
(Sometimes a dream-catcher will need to ask a dreamer if they can identify with how they are like a cow, using the description they have already volunteered. This dreamer, however, had already worked on dreams previously and understood the importance of what she was saying as she said it.)

Be the dog.
[As Judith] *"I'm about to get closer to the bunker to investigate the plight of the cows when two vicious dogs chase me away."*

"I am a guard dog and I don't want you to go near that bunker."

Many of us will viciously resist anyone (even ourselves) getting closer to an injured or protected part of ourselves. Sometimes it is only through dreams that we can get close enough to realize what we are doing. This moving back and forth between the protagonists of the dream allows the dreamer to feel the full extent of their dilemma. In the context of a dream session, and within a supportive group, an experienced dreamer can be encouraged to "act into" the various characters and aspects of a dream in order to fully feel and identify the parts of themselves that they may have shut away for some time.

How are you going to escape?
"I remember getting down on all fours and roaring for help in a high-pitched moo. The dog came to my aid after I convinced him that he too was in a sorry state without his coat of hair. Using a mechanical digger, he knocked a hole in the concrete bunker for the cows to escape."

In this description Judith has "dreamed up" several reflections of her "sorry state", and when she puts them together, a creative solution presents itself. The dog is free and can ask for help, showing that part of her, although also in difficulties, is not totally shut away – it can call for help.

When working with a dream, remember that anything is possible. You are engaging with the creative process, the same process that created the dream in the first place. If, when identifying with a dream, you free-associate a mechanical digger, then your creativity is to be applauded.

In looking later at what a mechanical digger could actually be for her, Judith came to understand the power and strength that she needed to call on from within herself and from others in order to break free of the old pattern that kept her shut away and oblivious to what she really needed or felt.

The dream illustrated that it was not by chance that she had chosen to work with others who severely deprived themselves. Making the link, Judith was relieved to note how far she had moved on from her own desperate need to control and isolate herself.

"This dream-work had a dramatic effect on me. I became aware of how I was starving myself in my life. In fact, I was shocked that I was so self-abusive. This dream told my story in images to which I relate deeply, particularly as I had grown up in the 1980s when hunger strikes were often part of protests. After the dream-work, I vowed to take better care of myself.

"This dream has stayed alive for me in that when from time to time I have an image of a herd of cows needing to be put out to pasture to feed, I know I must take better care of myself. I'm grateful to my unconscious for illustrating my inner turmoil in such graphic form. A few years on

now, the glamour of starvation has worn off. I no longer pride myself on being able to survive so efficiently. I am less prone to shutting the world out and just existing. My concrete bunker is now a haven in times of deep distress, which, needless to say, are now rare."

Personal behaviours often arise not just out of habit, but out of need. These survival behaviours cannot simply be put aside or stepped over. As with any defensive structure, they were put there for a reason, and even if the defence subsequently becomes an obstacle to the way we want to live, it cannot just be dismantled.

Preparation for change

We take the first step towards change when we recognize from our dreams that the way we are behaving is not serving us well. In dreams we are usually operating with the same complement of habitual feelings and reactions that we bring to our waking life. However, there is always something or someone in our dreams who illustrates another possibility.

You will already have discovered and (we hope) identified with the different parts and characters of your dream. Are you willing to accept how you are like all these different parts? If there is a particular aspect or character in a dream that you just cannot identify with, you might find it helpful to imagine how your life would be if you allowed yourself to behave in that way.

Notice your resistant feelings. Do you have any rules about behaving in this way? If we persistently restrict our lives by trying to obey rules that once kept us safe but now no longer serve us, our dreams will start to present the forbidden behaviour to us, giving us a chance to re-evaluate our rigidity.

Honour the old ways

Despite the promptings of your dreams, it isn't easy to change survival patterns. They are habitual behaviours arising from family experiences. They have been honed by your life lessons. They serve a purpose and must be respected for the function they have had; only then will they start to loosen their grip on you and allow you to take the risk of behaving differently. It is important not just to try to stop an old behaviour, but to recognize the value that it has had for you. For example, looking after others is a caring and useful thing to do – it gives a good feeling and sometimes even a purpose for living. However, if you do it habitually without regard for your own emotional or physical well-being, your do-gooding can unreasonably restrict your life.

Sometimes, although you know the changes you need to make, you might feel awkward about making them. This is where working with a dream in a group of friendly strangers, all of whom are learning and making changes for themselves, can help you. In a group you will be encouraged to experiment with and test new behaviours before you venture to exercise them for real.

Making the changes

It is important not to expect too much from yourself too soon. Your consciousness has already been irrevocably changed by your dream-work. Your old self-defeating patterns are already loosening, yet you might feel fragile and unsupported – even embarrassed – about behaving differently. At first, just notice how you now see things differently. Don't jump into the change; if you do, be prepared to be a bit over the top. It is natural to swing to the opposite pole in order to get rid of what you now know to be self-destructive. Making changes externally requires courage as well as will-power. Practise privately in your thoughts for a while. Note to yourself how you would prefer to behave, or what other options you might wish to exercise. Rehearsing possibilities in your mind will ease you into change.

Remember that awareness is an incurable disease, so you have plenty of time to practise. Let loved ones know about your new perspective and tell them that you are wanting to change but that old habits die hard. Even though your dreams may have provided an insight that has profoundly changed your perspective overnight, behavioural change will happen more gradually. When you first become aware, you may be surprised or even shocked. You will inevitably see your behaviour in a new light. Determined to change, you proceed, only to fall back into the old patterns, especially during times of stress, tiredness or excitement. But now you know what you are doing, your awareness will eventually catch up with you. Just as you are about to react in a self-defeating way, you will be able to stop yourself. Remember that progress is different for everyone. Take your time and your dreams will continue to show you the way forward.

It may be quite a challenge to return to familiar surroundings and make the changes there, where you might meet the resistance of colleagues, friends and family who will all be affected by your decision to do things differently. It sometimes turns out that you are the last one to have recognized the need for change. Usually, those close to you will be delighted with your new style, and happy to see you looking after yourself so well.

Dreams not only show the things you may need to do for yourself. Your unconscious may pick up a great deal of information about others and your surroundings. Sometimes a dream may accurately sum up a relationship, a family situation or a group, as the following example shows.

A FREEZING RECEPTION

After the first session of an analytic group, a new member dreamt that she was in a large commercial kitchen, all stainless steel and tiled floors, cold and impersonal. The kitchen seemed empty, and when she opened the doors of the large refrigerators and freezers, she saw that they were stuffed full of game: pheasant, partridge, hare and venison. In the dream she wanted to thaw out all the game and have a banquet. When she returned to the next session of the group with this dream, it gave the group conductor an opportunity to comment on the group process and the members' frosty response to the newcomer. He challenged them all to own their "game". The telling of the dream went some way towards breaking the ice.

Of course, this dream, as well as representing what the dreamer felt about the group, was symbolic of herself. It represented her own coldness and isolation. (She had been brought up around industrial kitchens as both her parents were cooks. Her unconscious reaction to the group was a re-run of her past experiences of being sidelined in the kitchen.) She had judged the group negatively and challenged them to be different, rather than recognizing that maybe she could learn to fit in.

Dreams reflect how we live together

Everyday relationships inspire dreaming, and it follows that dreams will affect our everyday relationships. Sadly, in the same way that some people are unable to speak from their heart, many people feel unable to share their dreams with their partners. Sharing an unworked dream with someone who is unfamiliar with unconscious processes could invite misunderstanding. Dreams can reflect in symbolic form the underlying truth of a relationship, and presents facts about which you may already have some inkling, but might not really want to know about.

Most of us are pleased if a partner or friend dreams about us, especially in a flattering light. It means we have significance for them. Even if a comparative stranger dreams of us positively or romantically, we feel flattered. Sharing such dreams can enable us to come closer. If, however, we are dreamt of in a violent, hostile or disgusting role, we are less likely to want to hear about it. A member of a monthly dream-catching group had the following dream.

JOY'S DREAM
"The TV is on in the room, but I decide to read and choose from a pile of children's books. I pick one that has buttons to press so it talks to you. Someone was reading it earlier and I could hear it, but I wanted to read it for myself. Then someone (I don't know who, or where they come from) tells me, 'It's not a very good book. Don't read that, and anyway, it's dirty.' I don't quite know whether they mean physically dirty or pornographic. I think they mean physically, but I can't actually see anything wrong with it and I'm puzzled. Then it occurs to me that they mean it's got loads of germs on it. I feel frightened, so I put the book down, even though I'd like to read it, and wake up."

What would you like to do now?
"I want to work the dream, but I feel very nervous about working it, very scared. It feels very big and deep and I really need to feel safe to work it."

How are you going to get safe?
"I need to look at you all. I'm remembering that we've worked on dreams before where I've felt very scared and I've been fine with you. I know that you've worked with dreams that you felt scared about... I'm feeling calmer now."

So where would you like to begin? In which part of the dream are you most interested?
"It was actually the book."

Be the book; we don't know what a book is.

"I'm a flat, hard thing and I have wonderful treasures inside. I'm exciting and I've got pictures and words, so all sorts of people can get pleasure from me. I don't have to be only for certain types of people and I've even got talking words. I've got written and talking words so that young children can hear me even if they can't read, which I think is lovely. I like that about me. And I'm a positive book – a fairy tale or something to teach people with, but also light-hearted... something... [choking a little and crying] *I have a light-heartedness inside me and I don't let it out very often.* [Pause] *I know someone has put Joy off looking at me and I'm cross about that. She hasn't made up her own mind about me."*

As the book, talk to Joy or the person who put her off, or both of them.

"This is the person and that's Joy [indicating two cushions]. *I want to say to the person, 'Why are you telling Joy not to read me and that I'm dirty? It's not up to you to tell her; it's up to her to make up her own mind. And actually I'm cross with you and you* [Joy] *too because you just accepted what this person said about me – you didn't find out for yourself. I'm disgusted that you just accepted what they said. I don't expect that of you. You're bigger than that. You're old enough to make up your own mind and I'm hurt that you would just take what they say and not investigate for yourself.* [Pause]

[Joy as herself] *"I've got some feeling here that I can't describe very easily. In some way I feel bigger, but also as if there's a lump. As I was saying truthfully how angry I was, I felt bigger. But there's also this very tight lump inside."*

(When a dreamer becomes conscious of their body language, such as twisting the hands or biting the lip, or notices a physical sensation, the dream-catching focus needs to move – to the physical activity, for example.)

Speak from the lump.

"I'm a tight lump inside Joy, sitting in the middle of her chest near her heart, hanging on tight. I can feel my teeth gritting. [She burps – often a sign that something is moving deeply inside.] *I'm making myself smaller and smaller because I am hanging on so tight."*

What's your need to hang on so tight?
[Burps again] *"If I hang on tight, I don't have to do anything else, be any other way. I can just hang on, not feel. I can not feel."*

(When a dreamer is holding on to something – a physical position or life stance – it is important not to push him or her in another direction or suggest alternatives. Just accepting that what is going on has a purpose will allow the dreamer to relax and explore what they are doing. Remember that change only truly happens when we fully accept how we are and what we are dealing with. The dream-catcher knowing this confirms and reflects back to the dreamer what he or she is saying.)

So, even though there's a part of Joy that's got bigger and is clearly saying that it feels misused and misjudged, there is also another part that is hanging on?
"Mmm…"

If that's what you want to do, that's all right – you can keep hanging on until you are ready to let go. You still seem able to operate around this old pattern.
"I feel safe, I don't want anyone to come near or touch me." [Silence, then Joy grimaces]

What's your thought?
"I'm reminded of a piece of work that someone did where they were afraid to be touched in case they'd die. I don't feel sure I'd die, but I know I don't want to be touched. I just want to shrink and be small and not noticed. [Tearful] When they did that piece of work, I didn't feel anything at all."

And now?
[Crying] *"I hurt and it doesn't matter if I hold on or not. It's not going to go away."*
(She now faces this fact – her feelings contracted into the lump can now be felt and recognized.)

Look at me and say the whole thing.
"I'm hurting and I'm holding on and I don't want you to touch me."

Because if I touched you?

"I might break…mmm… Someone did touch me at the weekend and I got very scared. I don't feel so bad now I've said that."

(Now the real-life connection is made.)

I notice your words. You don't feel so bad, and we're looking at this book being bad and dirty, not to be read, dangerous.

"Yes, as you say that, I really hurt in my heart."

So there is part of you that can stand up and say, "Don't talk badly of me, or listen to people who talk badly about me. How come you listen to them?" And you are big enough to face this. Yet there's another part of you that shrivels and feels hurt and may not be touched.

"Yes. I'm very scared of being seen. And I also know that I need contact and it's impossible to get contact without being seen."

(She is now accepting how she behaves along with its consequences.)

The dream-catcher now refers back to the dream in order to use other parts that could help move her client on.

That's right, otherwise you are not in contact. Let's stay with your dream. We've got some sense of the book now. Let's hear from the two people in the dream.

[As Joy] *"I'm interested in you and I was put off you by what this person said. I didn't want to be…contaminated. And I was scared of germs. I can't afford to be ill. In real life I can't afford to be ill and I don't want to risk catching anything, so I'm not going to take the risk."*

Penny drop?

"Not quite there yet, I'm getting there… Yes! The penny's dropped. [Laughs and continues excitedly] I am immensely interested to read you. You are exciting and intriguing and I know I can learn a lot from you. [Quietly] And I'm scared of being judged according to who you are."

Who are you speaking to?

(Here she is invited to make the link with a real person, not just the book.)

"Steven."

You are talking to Steven and you are also talking to that part of yourself that is like him.
"Yes."

Be this person in the dream who warned you off.
"What are you doing reading that book, Joy? [In a panicky voice] *Don't touch that book. That book's not right. It's dirty. I don't think you should read it, just put it down and leave it alone. It's not safe."*
[As Joy, firmly and quietly] *"I know it's not safe, and I can look after myself."*

What about the germs?
"Mmm, well... I'm hesitating because I'm trying not to think, but to feel. What I feel when I think about the book is that it's inherently a good thing and yes, there is a risk of catching something, but if I spend my whole life not in contact with people for fear of that risk, I'm going to stay alone."

Let's get something straight here. Let's use the symbolism of your dream. There is a book that's dirty, but you don't know in what way, so you err on the side of caution and put that book down. What would you do if you were really in that situation?
"I suppose I need to check what is meant by dirty. [To warning person in dream] *Yes, what do you mean by dirty, because I'm not sure what you mean. Is it jam, is it germs, is it sex or pornography, what is it?"*
[As the warning person] *"It's a children's book, definitely, so it isn't pornographic. It's sticky, it's sticky!"*

So who are you to protect Joy by judging this book in the dream?
"Oh! I'm your mother when you were little. I was telling you that it was sticky, you'd get your hands dirty before you went to bed. You'd get it all over the sheets and I'd have to wash them. I was trying to save myself a job."
[As Joy] *"Well, first of all I am an adult (that's why I was confused about the word dirty: it seemed so inappropriate for a children's book), so I can get sticky hands and I can go and wash them. I am old enough to know that and I won't go to bed with sticky hands. And you haven't got to*

wash the bloody sheets anyway. It's someone else's house. I'm devastated that I listened to you so easily. I just let you walk all over me. I suppose that's what I've done all my life – tried to be a good girl."

Switch back to talking to Mum now.
"Now, Mum – I am an adult, not a child, and actually this book – it's a person – it's Steven."

Now, as Mum, try saying to her, "Don't get all sticky on the sheets."
[As mother, horrified] *"I can't say that to her. I'm her mother. I can't talk about that sort of thing."*

So there is a part of you, Joy, that is like your mother trying to keep you a good, clean girl. You tell Joy of the danger in this way by making Steve into a story book. And now it's clear that the dirtiness is stickiness and the risk of disease. We can see that this is also an adult warning, so now be an adult mother (not your original mother) and say, "Listen, Joy, if you are going to take this book to bed with you… "
"If you are going to take this book to bed with you, it's like this – there's good and bad about it. You run the risk of pregnancy for a start, possibly disease, but on the other hand, you might have a wonderful time and not have either of those other things happen to you… as long as you are aware of what you are doing and how you are doing it and are taking precautions."
[As Joy] *"I am aware and I am taking precautions. It's not like teenagers fumbling about and not being able to talk to each other. We do talk."*
[Pause]

Though?
"Um… we did have an accident at the weekend."

Even though you take precautions? When did you have the dream?
"Friday night."

Before the accident? Your subconscious was trying to tell you something. They say if you have a dream where your car wheel falls off, or your brakes don't work, check your car. Unconsciously, you may be picking up something that indicates the wheel is not all right. I am interested in the timing of this dream.

"I was thinking – Steven and I had a conversation about whether we want a child. Neither of us is sure, but we think while we're not sure, we will be careful, which feels right."
[As Joy in dream] *"Hello, book. [Smiling] I love books."*

Can you say I love you to Steven?
"I love you."

You look sad.
"Because I want him to tell me he loves me too."

Look at this book: it has pictures and when it describes itself here, it tells you clearly, "There is part of me that I am holding on to and I don't want touched – a part of me that is hurt." This book represents both you and Steven, so now can you say I love you.
"Yes, Steven, I love you and I know you love me (because you've said it once) and I suffer when I start expecting you to tell me instead of trusting."

What would you say to Steven now?
"We are both incredibly alike, and I feel I really exposed myself at the weekend. I feel really scared and from hearing this book speak in my dream, it seems that this is where you are too. I feel OK with that. I don't want to rush you and I don't want you to rush me."

(The dream-catcher, being familiar with the progression of Steven and Joy's love affair, takes a liberty.)
Perhaps the reason that Steven is so attractive to you is that he is big enough to say, "Make up your mind, be an adult." There is also this part inside both of you that's hurt. You are in some ways both the same – both big enough to say, "Hold off," but not yet safe enough to truly let go, to be touched.
"I can't go around berating you [Steven] for being like that when I am exactly the same."

Be the book/Steven.
"Well, thank God you worked on this dream! I feel really solid here. This is who I really am."

Make it explicit.
"Who I really am is…a book with interesting pages and a hard, tight lump inside that is very vulnerable. It's hard to look at you."

So rather than striving to touch each other, can you just settle for how you are at present?
"Yes."

No amount of reassurance from another is going to stop you holding on. You have to do that from the inside.
"True."

Sharing dreams can give couples an opportunity to re-evaluate how they are with each other. Dreams or dream-catching are not the cause of discomfort – they simply shine a light on the discomfort that is already there. Many couples unconsciously push each other into relationship polarities ("She's the articulate one, he's the practical one," for example). If one partner is holding back emotional responses, even more pressure will be put on the other partner to exhibit or express that emotion. It is quite common to witness one partner carrying all the aggression while their mate plays the role of peace-maker. The talkative one may be paired with the silent or quiet "other half". The reason one person may appear to have exaggerated responses could be because they are having to carry more than their share of the partnership's vulnerability or aggression. Ideally, each person will eventually come to own their full complement of emotional responsiveness. Dreams can help in this task.

The inhibitions you have accumulated throughout your upbringing and socialization have only a very light hold on your dream world. In your dreams you can exercise your full repertoire of intellectual and emotional responses. What is consciously forbidden will inevitably arise within your dreams in one form or another. Through dream-catching you may experience and experiment with new ways of being. Then, having rehearsed within safe bounds, you can take the choice to become more authentic and less inhibited in real life.

CHAPTER 5

At times a dream may provoke old terrors. Dream-catching makes it possible to discover what they might be referring to in real life. It could be an opportunity to lay old ghosts to rest and re-evaluate an old survival pattern. Perhaps you are being given an opportunity to say to others in your past what you needed to say to them way back then, but couldn't. Reliving dreams might make old hurts reappear, but this time you are different. Take the new perspective your dream is showing you and do it your way.

TONI'S DREAM

A shy woman in her early thirties, Toni had joined a dating agency. Having met several possible partners, she started a relationship with David, whom she found to be kind, considerate and tender, as well as good company. In the early days of the relationship, she held her boundaries, setting her own pace. She then had the following dream.

"I am on a train and the doors won't let me off at the stop I need. I wait for the next stop. but once again the doors stay shut. Eventually, the doors open at a station that is unfamiliar to me. It is dusk and I have to walk quite a way to where I see some lights. As I am walking, I notice a man who seems to be limping, following me. He comes right up to me and is very interested in me. I back away from him and he follows me into a corner. I know this dream is really important for me to work with, especially now that I am in a relationship with a man that I really like."

Be the limping man.
"Well, I'm not very attractive and I'm a bit slow and simple. I see this lovely woman and I want to get to know her but she seems really frightened of me."

What's happening with you?
"I feel really sad. All she needs to say is stop, and I'll go away. She doesn't have to be so afraid of me. I don't want to hurt her. I just like her."

(Despite being an attractive young woman, here Toni got in touch with her feelings of not being acceptable or pretty. She remembered her father saying in front of her to her mother, "She really isn't that attractive." She now wept for the cruelty of it and the pain he had caused her.)

Be Toni in the dream.
"I got so scared. I thought he was going to come at me."

As she said these words she remembered how for many years she had barricaded her bedroom door for fear of her father coming in. He did not seem to recognize the father/daughter boundaries, and had often spoken salaciously to her and in her presence, as if she were just another woman to be seduced. She wept as she recalled how she had desperately tried to avoid drawing attention to herself, even making herself unattractive in order to keep the suggestive comments of her father and her brothers at bay. She had become fat and used to hiding herself away. She remembered that being sent to boarding school felt like a relief, as well as a punishment, because she no longer had to fend them off. She got in touch with her anger towards the men in her family and expressed her rage at how she had been treated, telling them to f*** off and leave her alone.

When her anger and tears were spent, Toni recognized more fully where her need to avoid relationships with men had come from. She saw how her need to control relationships and keep herself to herself was based on her familial experiences, and that the inhibitions she was feeling with David were deep-seated and belonged in her past. Realizing now that nothing was wrong with her, she saw that her reticence had been formed by habitual fear of invasion within her family. She wanted to be open and relaxed with her partner but had up to now instinctively shut off from him if he tried to make the pace. She laughed with relief at the prospect of becoming freer with him, at the thought of welcoming his passion, safe in the knowledge that he wasn't her father and that she could ask him to stop at any time.

As Toni worked with her dream, her face lit up and the full radiance of her womanliness and beauty shone through. She determined to give herself more space to allow her man to approach her, confident in the knowledge that she was no longer that terrified child or fat teenager. She could say no and have it heard. Even more importantly, she now was safe enough to say yes.

Such realizations are liberating, but old inhibitions persist and Toni knew from past experience that she must be kind and patient with herself as her instinctive defences would continue to operate. She now understood more fully what they were about and resolved to give herself and her partner as much time as they might need to dismantle the barricades.

Personal defences can cause difficulties within relationships, but when understood by both partners, there is a good chance of avoiding potential misunderstandings caused by them. Sadly, some weeks later Toni realized that David was not as committed as she, so the relationship broke up. However, despite her hurt and disappointment, she remains optimistic and has not retreated into her shell. She recognizes that what she learned from this relationship has been good practice for another that might last longer.

Most of us know that barricading ourselves into a safe place does not enable us to avoid pain. It merely snuffs the vitality out of our lives. Thankfully, we remain vitally alive within our dreams. They are a transformatory resource freely available to us all.

TAKING THE BULL BY THE HORNS

Elizabeth dreamt that she was lifted up between the horns of a gigantic bull who was travelling at speed. In the dream she knew she was in danger, but at the same time nothing bad was happening to her, so she started to enjoy the ride. She relaxed, knowing that she couldn't do anything but focus on staying balanced as the bull rushed her through the night. Eventually the bull stopped, lowered its head and gently deposited her back on the ground.

When she worked with the dream, Elizabeth recalled how she felt excited and uplifted, if a little frightened, and she made the connection to how she was feeling with her new partner. She decided to enjoy the energy between them and trust that she could have a safe landing.

Family "Therapy"

Sharing dreams can also benefit family relationships, especially when there are aspects of ourselves that we don't want to deal with directly for fear of causing upset or conflict. For example, a sixteen-year-old girl, sweet by nature and generally helpful, had been finding her mother's menopausal misery difficult to deal with. There seemed to be one crisis after another, and she was sick of having an unhappy mother around. After one difficult evening filled with silence, they went to bed. In the morning they greeted each other lightly, determined to be cheerful, and then the daughter told her about the following dream:

"I dreamt that I was here in the kitchen flicking ever larger portions of my muesli on to the floor. I was getting angrier and angrier, until I finally picked up the bowl and smashed it."

Mother: "What, one of my favourite bowls? [Mock horror] You were so angry with me yesterday that you would break my bowl?"

Then they both grinned at each other, glad to have broken only the painful silence between them. The mother knew about dreams and realized that her daughter was feeling a bit like both the muesli and the bowl – thrown on to the floor, even smashed and unable to contain "good stuff" any more. She came to understood more fully how her silence and unhappiness was having an impact on her daughter and resolved to protect her better in the future by not allowing her "downs" to intrude so much upon their life together. She resolved to seek more help from friends and partners, and perhaps look for some professional support in order to deal with her distress.

Dream insights can sometimes benefit the people around us. When we identify with the significant others in our dreams, we may come to recognize not only hidden aspects of ourselves, but also something of the other person's point of view.

Walking in another person's shoes

A dream is a template of a dreamer's unconscious processes. Although some of the characters in the dream may exist in real life, dreamers are using them onto which to project their own difficult, longed for, unwanted or fearful parts. For example, someone who is unable to be assertive might dream that their lover is killing them. This might be metaphorically true: the partner could indeed be more assertive or aggressive in real life. However, the dreamer needs to acknowledge their own aggression, the killer part of themselves. Dreams often present an exaggeration of suppressed anger or assertiveness and paste it on to a person who in reality is more comfortable with or capable of the characteristic than the dreamer.

MIRA'S DREAM

Helen's daughter, Mira, had been unhappy for some time about the work pressures on her life. She was feeling isolated and was also missing her school friends.

"I dreamt I was at the check-out of a French supermarket and I met up with some girls I used to be at school with. They were very friendly and wanted to chat and ask questions, although I was never really friendly with them before. I stayed for a bit and talked, then I remembered that Mum was waiting in the car for me. I rushed out to the car but my way was blocked by a guy on a scooter doing "wheelies" and showing off. He held out his hand for some money but I pushed past him and got into the car. Mum was annoyed with me for not giving him anything, and even more so when we started to drive off and she noticed the bloke on the scooter in front of the car. There was lots of space in the car park, but she drove straight into him and he ended up spreadeagled over the windscreen. She reversed back suddenly and left him lying on the ground, all the time blaming me for not having given him what he wanted."

Despite the fact that the dream was quite an accurate description of how irritated Helen did get with her when she dawdled, Mira could see how it was she who was frustrated in real life because she had no time to socialize. She was missing her friends and she was angry and impatient when she couldn't join in the fun. At first, she didn't think about identifying with the lad on the scooter. Then, when she did, she started to laugh. It was a part of herself that needed support (a hand-out) to freewheel around and have fun. The part of her that was represented in the dream by her mother was just so angry at not having any fun that she felt like killing it off by running it over and dumping it.

Nonsense dreams

Sigmund Freud said that "Dreams are often most profound when they seem the most crazy." Look at any paradoxical circumstance in a dream as if it has its own rhyme and reason. Eventually, all will become clear. The bizarreness of a dream has a purpose. For example, it might make you look anew at a familiar object, or search your heart and mind to discover how you are contorting the truth.

DUNCAN'S LEMMING DREAM

A radio presenter tried out dream-catching before interviewing Helen for his show. He had dreamt of lemmings – hundreds and hundreds of them – flooding towards a cliff edge. He had stood with a companion, watching as they tumbled over the edge, but noticed that some of them fell for a bit, then flew up and out of danger's way. He was puzzled by this dream, so Helen asked him to be a lemming and describe himself:

"I am a small, soft creature and I've got wings. I am rather timid and don't really take any risks or think for myself."

(Here Helen recognized that he wasn't describing any ordinary lemming, but rather than disturb his train of thought, she said nothing.)

And in this dream?
"I am following everyone else and they are taking me over the edge."
[Sounds anxiously excited as he recognizes himself and his predicament.]

And what about the ones that fly?
"Oh, yes, of course…I've got wings, I can fly. If I flap my wings, I can fly." [Great relief and excitement]

How are you like this?
"Well, I do tend to follow rather than going my own way. And everybody tells me that I could go further than I am letting myself. I could fly!"

Tell me again about lemmings.
"Oh, these aren't lemmings, are they? They've got wings!"

Perhaps you are not a lemming after all?
"I've always thought of myself as a lemming…when, in fact, I'm a bird."
[Great laughter and relief]

Let's go to your companion in the dream. Has he got anything to say to you?
"He's an older, wiser man… a bit like a mentor. He says, 'I've brought

you here to see your history. You do not have to be like this. You can be different'."

Tell me what in your history is like these lemmings following to their death, not taking the risks to go their own way.
"Oh, my father! He follows along, never takes risks. Perhaps this means that I don't have to be like him."

Duncan resolved to follow his dreams more. He was coming up for a job review and decided really to go for the change he wanted.

The ability to weave from one reality to another, to focus on the dream and yet access common sense and creativity from the real world, can give vital clues to the dreamer. To think laterally is the mark of innovators and creators. It is a skill that improves with practice.

There is truth within dreams. When dreamers make a connection through hearing themselves use a particular phrase or tone of voice, everything may suddenly shift into a different perspective. A gestalt (something striving for completion) may be closed and the way forward may become clear.

In the early stages of dream-catching, the ability to work with a dream in this way may not yet be developed. A dreamer may jump to conclusions about images and make assumptions about their meanings. Short-circuiting the dream-work in this way can lead to frustration; the dreamer may feel stuck and become discouraged from exploring further.

Within a dream there will always be clues about the situation you must attend to – how you feel about it and how you could potentially improve it. To discover these clues you must turn the various pieces of your dream over and identify with each one, giving it a voice. Sometimes you might need to follow this formula for only one or two aspects of the dream before you get the message. At other times, the dream wisdom seems too obscure and each part of the dream may need to be explored. You are connected to all the dream parts, whether you like them or not. Each represents a possibility for you. As one participant in a dream-catching workshop said, "It seems that I already have the answers: I just need to know how to ask the questions."

Useful dream-working questions
- How am I like this?
- When am I like this?
- What is my need to be like this?
- What will happen if I continue to be like this?
- What is my purpose?
- What do I need?
- Who do I need to say this to?

Pieces of your dream jigsaw can be rearranged to show different perspectives of the same scene. For example, using an open gate rather than pushing at a heavy door might show you how in real life you could get to the same place with less effort.

A dream is a wonderful three-dimensional play space within which you can manoeuvre and try out possibilities before taking any action in the real world. When you feel you have enough information, that the dream makes sense for you and you know what action is needed, ask yourself the following:

Useful questions after dream-working
- What will be the possible consequences if I do or don't do this?
- How would my life change if I let myself be this way?
- What support do I need to do this?

6

THE IMPACT
OF DREAMS

The purpose of this chapter is to show the power and breadth of possibilities within dream-catching. The following studies illustrate a wide range of issues and a variety of working styles. Choose whichever seems most relevant to you.

- Mira, a teenage girl searching for her father, learns to look after herself, confront her friends and confirm her identity.
- After one telephone session, twenty-something Scarlet begins to liberate herself from an old guilt and learns to work with her own dreams.
- Thirty-year-old Judith engages in a long process of reclaiming the fullness of her life after surviving a childhood of attacks and restrictions.
- Middle-aged Ivor starts to reconnect with his roots to gain emancipation from his parents.

Some dreamers, such as Judith, need to explore their dreams thoroughly in order to find a creative solution to their present dilemmas. Others, such as Mira, demonstrate that it is not essential to work each piece of a dream. Unravelling just a segment of a dream may be so rewarding that the rest of it (often a variation of the main theme anyway) may be left unworked. The section describing Scarlet's dream-catching mentions a dream-symbol interpretation that she got off the Internet. She ultimately found it more of a hindrance than a help, so decided to try the dream-catching process by herself, with interesting results. These examples illustrate that it really doesn't matter what part of the dream you start with; each part will lead to the dream's essential theme.

Mira

At sixteen, Mira decided to leave school and complete her GCSEs at evening classes so that she could take up an apprenticeship in stable management and riding. After spending a hard year juggling studies, horse work and waitressing at a pub, she was feeling both exhausted and trapped. Although her exams were over, her commitments to the stable and waitressing were intensifying. The year had shown her that although she loved riding, she did not want a career as a horsewoman: she wanted to return to school to study for A levels. However, leaving school early had taken a toll, and she now felt very much outside her previous social circle. While many of her friends were planning exciting holidays, she was struggling to negotiate extra help at the stables, but to no avail. All those around her could see that she was very tired and distressed.

Helen was worried about her, but Mira didn't want to talk, saying that it put her under yet more pressure. She knew that something had to go; her dilemma was that she didn't want to let down either the stables or the pub. During her exams, while she wasn't earning, she had been borrowing from Helen, but now she wanted to start paying Helen back as well as having some money for herself. Mira knew that she should continue with the stables and give up the waitressing, but the stables were expensive and she was no longer enjoying the work. She had managed through a long hard winter and now felt enough was enough. During this struggle Helen had stood back (with some difficulty), respecting Mira's need to negotiate her own life. Now she could see her daughter heading for a breakdown of sorts, so she stepped in and offered to negotiate on her behalf. Mira confided that she had been feeling so desperate that she had even thought of running away. The next night she had a dream.

MIRA'S FIRST DREAM

"In the dream I have three boyfriends, all of whom I have been able to keep apart up to a big event, a ball, that they all think they are taking me to. I'm walking through this building and I don't seem to feel anything, although I am aware of the inevitable difficulty I'll have to face. Then I am walking down the track to the ponies. There are a group of my friends behind me, all going somewhere, and I am hurrying ahead of them so I can see to my ponies and still have enough time to catch them up. Across the path is a fallen tree or bush. I go straight into it and it's full of bees. I am shocked and afraid but not stung, and I try to brush them all away. I carry on, only to be faced with another tree/bush full of bees which I have to go through. Then I hear someone calling me and I see a hand waving to the side and realize it's the people behind me who have caught up on a parallel path. That path is clear and I can't understand why I have chosen the hard path and kept to it. I was even going to go through the second bush of bees.

"Then I am in Sparrow's Lodge [the old family home] *and there is a man, an older man, chasing me and I'm sure he is going to attack me, rape me, and I am really frightened. I run from him into the house but he won't leave me alone. I try to get him to back off but he keeps on*

coming. I grab a big knife and I stab at him, but he keeps coming, so I have to cut him up into little bits. I am really upset and feel sick at what I've done, and rush to find you. You are with a group of strangers. When I tell you, nobody thinks that what I've done is bad, but instead of feeling comforted, I feel that none of you really understands and that I am unsupported – as if my feelings of guilt are being dismissed."

OK. What do you make of this?
"Well, I guess the three boyfriends are like my three lives – the horses, the pub and my studies – and I can't keep them separate any more. I do know this feeling of just trudging on down the path through whatever obstacle is in front of me. It's so stupid when I really knew there was another way. I just needed someone else to encourage me to take it."

What about the old guy?
"I'm just so terrified and afraid, but when I woke up I was amazed that I could kill like that. I guess I have felt really angry but had nowhere to put it. And I guess that's why I wanted to run away. I could murder everybody."

Be Sparrow's Lodge.
"I am a beautiful open house [pauses, welling up with tears] *and I'm empty."* [Sobs as she realizes this is how she feels.]

What I can't understand is why didn't you lock the doors against him.
"That's not the sort of house I am."

How are you like Sparrow's Lodge, Mira? Wide open, beautiful and empty, not willing or able to lock the doors?
(Mira weeps again at recognizing how hard it has been to say no and keep herself safe.)

And you are not feeling comforted at the end?
"Well, it's as if nobody realizes what a bad thing I've done. They don't realize how bad I feel. Even you don't."

Helen telephoned the stables. It turned out the owners were already worried about Mira. They had been discussing her situation and suggested she should take a three-week break before making a decision about her future there. Mira was very relieved and over the next twenty-four hours her smile came back. She was on holiday (well, almost), having decided to keep waitressing for three days a week in order to pay her debts and save some money for a proper break away. She stayed in the staff flat each week, which improved her social life and gave her some freedom from home as well. She insisted that Helen should not cancel her debts (she needed not to feel obligated and guarded her independence fiercely).

Mira didn't pursue the other aspects of her dream as she was already full with the meanings she had uncovered so far. Later, she looked at the bees, the fallen tree/bush and also her friends. Identifying with these helped her to regain her confidence.

When working with young people, it is important to recognize the gift they are giving you: they are taking you into their confidence and showing you their innermost thoughts and needs. They are reaching out and revealing precious things that may be impossible for them to talk about in any other way. They need you to be sensitive, respect their privacy and not insist that they work out all their dream. Trust them to know when they have had enough.

MIRA'S SECOND DREAM

This dream demonstrates how, on another occasion, Mira's dreaming gave her the opportunity to own feelings that she had been persuaded to put away.

The previous year she had been late getting to an overnight party. When she arrived, she joined her boyfriend and her best friend, who were sitting together. She didn't think anything of it until others at the party told her that these two had been sitting on each other's knees and generally flirting with each other for the whole evening.

When she confronted them and asked what was going on, they both insisted that it was all innocent and that she had nothing to worry about, that she was being paranoid. She accepted their explanation, but a couple of days later, while travelling to school, she told Helen about a dream. (The school drive is often an opportunity to share dreams as Helen's need to concentrate on the road allows Mira to work on her dreams with some privacy. Even so, there are times after telling a dream when Mira will keep a distance by saying, "Look I know what it means" or "I don't want to work on this." In the following case, she did choose to look more deeply into her dream.

"I am with the gang and they are all saying that my mother is crazy, a bit weird. I feel hurt and don't know how to answer them. I want to be with them and join in the fun, but I feel out of it and can't understand why they are insulting my mother in this way."

What's a mother?
"A mother sort of looks after children."

How are you like that?
"Well, I guess I do look after everybody a bit. Sometimes I feel older than them."
(Mira is one year older than most of her classmates, having "lost" a year of schooling while living in France. Her five years abroad do sometimes make her appear older than her years.)

OK, be the mother.
"These kids are poking fun at me and thinking I'm a bit weird. I don't really care because they don't know what they are talking about. Anyway, I know that I'm all right. There's nothing wrong with me."

How are you like that Mira?
"Well, I do know that there's nothing wrong with me, and no matter what they say, it's not me that's crazy. [Pause] Oh! This is how I was feeling at the party when I asked them what was going on. I felt as if they were making out that I was crazy, and I know I'm not. It's what they were doing that's not OK. Everyone saw them but they made me out to be in the wrong for challenging them. Oh, I feel so angry!"

Mira went to school and confronted her friend and boyfriend, and with the support of her other friends, they sorted it out. There were a few tears and a bit more heartache, but she no longer felt stupid or crazy.

If your children ask you to work with their dreams, don't get hooked up with their storylines. For example, you might feel offended that even in a dream your child's friends think you are crazy. Keep that to yourself. It's your child's dream, every part of it is part of them. Let them work it out for themselves. Hold back your associations, just ask the question, "How are you like this?"

MIRA'S THIRD DREAM

One summer Mira contacted her father, who had never previously been a part of her life. She tracked down his number and telephoned him, heart in mouth. She managed to speak to him several times during the holiday and he was always very friendly and open with her, not at all rejecting, saying that he would meet her after his holiday, but that he needed to tell his new wife. He telephoned Mira as soon as he returned, saying that he had tried to tell his wife about her several times, but had bottled out at the last minute. He was sorry and said he would see her anyway if she wanted that. She was pleased that he had rung her and felt his sincerity, so she chose not to make his life difficult. She said she could wait. Now it was almost a year later and Mira still had no news from him. Again, she chose to tell this dream whilst travelling in the car.

"I dreamt that I have had my kneecap shot off and it has been stitched together quite roughly. I tell people about it and they are sympathetic, but now, although it's much later, it's still hurting me. It's just as sore as when I first mentioned it, yet I feel I can't say anything more about it as people will be impatient and bored with me. Nobody seems interested, or even notices that I am in pain. The pain is really bad."

Identifying with the kneecap, she said:
"I am the part that joins together the top and bottom of a leg. This is an old injury. I am the joining part and the whole leg can't work properly without me. I am the shock-absorber that protects the delicate joint and allows flexibility and movement. I am also a vital connection if the leg is to support Mira properly." [Looks thoughtful as what she is saying starts to sink in.]

Be the leg.
"A part of me is smashed up and missing. My shock-absorber has gone. I am hurting, I am sore, but I am still expected to function properly. But I can't. I am in pain." [Tears roll down her cheeks.]

What do you need?

"I need attention and care. I need somebody to do something to help me work properly and take away the pain. [Quietly crying] *I don't feel very safe. I need my kneecap. I feel disconnected."*

As Mira talked, she realized that this was exactly how she was feeling – as if her missing father had been "shot away", an old injury that no longer deserved attention. She felt that no one else noticed her pain about his absence – that she should have got over it by now, that it was not OK for her to be still hurting about it. No one was noticing that the part of her that could absorb the shock was missing.

At this point, Helen, although driving the car, was able to reach out a hand and give Mira some of the sympathy and recognition she needed. Later, when they talked again, Mira expressed more fully her frustration and hurt with the situation. It was that precious moment of realization in the car, however, that had given her the most relief and had prompted Helen to reach out to her.

Teenagers are often awkward about touch, and may barricade the intensity of their feelings behind high walls. When they break through to you with a dream, savour the moment and resist the temptation to make too much of it.

After Mira read this script and gave her permission for it to be published, she said: "It is really amazing. I have no idea of the actual meaning of these dreams when I am working with them, or how they relate to my life. And sometimes, even when working through the dream, it doesn't come to me straight way. When I work with you, you know some of the things that are happening in my life and can ask the right questions. The most powerful thing is, when I'm talking about it and suddenly I hear myself and it hits me. I wasn't even thinking about my friends or my dad at the time. Although both times I was feeling a bit down."

Scarlet

Following a free telephone dream consultation offered by Dream Catchers, twenty-something Scarlet wrote to Helen about a recurrent dream involving her first serious boyfriend. She described their relationship as the most significant of her life.

SCARLET'S FIRST DREAM

"I am dreaming all the time about my first love and his new wife. He and I are standing in Sloane Square. We are holding hands and have no shoes on, which feels quite comfortable and natural – liberating. All around are really tall glass buildings, and his parents are having lunch in one of them. He is pulling me towards them and I am feeling really frightened and scared, knowing that they will question me about why I left him. I wake up, then dream again that he is married to a friend who is pregnant and I am on the floor reaching up to them, crying and screaming for help, but she's lecturing me to pull myself together. Then they shut the door on me."

Working on the telephone with Helen, Scarlet identified with each part of her dream in turn. After working through it, she realized that although she and her ex-boyfriend, Michael, have been parted for some time now, his constant appearances in her dreams are relevant to her life now. She still hasn't managed to deal with the guilt she feels at leaving him. Helen suggested that she have an imaginary conversation with Michael. It unfolded like this:

"I'm sorry I left you in that way. I was so young and naive. I needed to become my own person. I had been with you so long, and Phillip [the new boyfriend] *excited me. I felt lonely in the relationship I had with you. Even though we had many friends, they were not really there for you and me. They were there for the lifestyle and what your money offered them. I needed my own friends. All the money in the world wouldn't have made our relationship good. I needed to leave you, so I went off with Phillip and I had a good time."*

[As Michael] *"I can understand your doing that, wanting that, but why in someone else's arms? You used me and I feel bad."*

"I needed to be a whole person rather than an appendage to your life. I needed to be liked for me. I was very lucky to be with you, but felt I had no independence and I thought perhaps I never would, living the way we did."

CHAPTER 6

[As Michael] *"I wanted to spoil you so much that no man would ever be as good as me."*

"I would like to get on with my life now without blaming myself or needing to take you into it."

[As Michael] *"Well, I have my life with my wife now."*

At this point Scarlet came back to the reality. This imaginary conversation helped her to finish her business with her ex-lover. It left her feeling tearful but relieved to understand what her recurrent dreams were about.

SCARLET'S SECOND DREAM
Three days after our first session, Scarlet sent me an e-mail:

"I don't really know where to start after such an emotional telephone conversation, but thank you for helping me to understand and release myself from the past. Since then I have been through quite a lot of different emotions, from sadness to happiness to relief. On Saturday night I wrote a letter [to Michael], as you suggested, then burnt it with a photo of the pair of us. I really think it worked. I dreamt something very different that night and would like to share it with you.

"I am a small child with amazing golden blonde hair. (As you know, I am naturally dark and Mediterranean-looking.) I am wearing a very pretty pinafore dress and sitting on a huge chair at an enormous table surrounded by the same kind of chairs. The table is set for a children's tea party, but I am alone. Then an adult pats me on the hair, saying, "You're such a good little girl." I am sitting there very comfortably, waiting to be told to start having tea, but quite happy with my own company. I smile when the adult reassures me, but in a childlike manner. The room is very dark, like a deep red, and there is a golden glow around me.

"Then the dream switches to me at home. In my downstairs cupboard I find a sort of cellar extension that I never knew. It leads into a huge Elizabethan-style room with very high and ornate wooden ceilings, stained-glass windows, embroidered carpets... Actually, it is more like a church and I am kneeling at some kind of altar and told to pick a ring

100

from a glass case. I go for a row of sapphires on rubies and emeralds. There are lots of stones but they are quite small and dull, although very strong colours. They are precious stones, I know that much. That's all I remember: just having to make a choice from the rings, and loving something about it, but choosing one that I wouldn't normally go for as my taste is usually quite loud and flashy.

"Since then I haven't dreamt of my ex, and for now that feels quite a relief – but I seem to up one minute and down the next."

Later, again on the telephone, Scarlet told Helen that she felt really wrung out and exhausted, and wondered why. Helen asked if she had mourned the loss of the relationship after leaving her boyfriend. (She had previously said that she had just got on with having a good time.) She said no, so Helen suggested that perhaps she was mourning now, which might be why she was feeling so sad and tired. Seven years of holding on was being released, and that hold on her feelings had taken a lot of energy. The whirl of activity and good times had distracted her from her feelings about Michael. This all made sense to Scarlet. They then worked on the follow-up dream.

Be the child at the table.
"I am a little golden girl, very innocent, very naive, very polite with a child's philosophy – patient, waiting to be told I can eat. I am very pleased and proud to be told that I am a very good girl. I like this confirmation that I am fine."

Be the table.
"I am a strong, sturdy table, simple, very rich wood, a deep colour, very polished. I am a foundation for everything that rests upon me. I hold everything together – like at Alice in Wonderland's tea party."

Be the person who reassures the little girl.
"It gives me so much pleasure to look at her and appreciate her. She's quite shy really, holding back."

[Scarlet as herself] *"I saw a friend on Monday and she noticed a change in me. She said whereas usually I would come in with a great whirl of energy around me, I was quieter and more level-headed, with no shrieking and laughter. She said that my insights and opinions were sound, whereas usually I would have run to everybody wanting conversation and confirmation."*

It's as if you now have a wider vocabulary?
"Yes. I'm not having to run away from seriousness."

Now be the cellar, the extra room in the dream.
"I am like a church. I have a wonderfully patterned floor with rich embroidered carpets and rich ceilings of oak, which point upwards, like a spire. I am a very big open space and my walls are a dirty golden sandstone. I am like a cross between a harem, an Elizabethan house and a church. [Laughs as she identifies with those parts of herself] Now I am a glass case and inside me is a selection of rings, all very different. Some are very ornate gemstones and they sparkle. There is a little one that hasn't been cleaned. It's very plain, a sort of dirty gold, and the ring doesn't quite meet in the middle. Scarlet looks at all the others – she usually goes for the eye-catcher – but she chooses the plain one."

[Scarlet as herself] *"This ring in the corner is quite quaint and attractive. It's pretty and would give me lots of pleasure. I feel drawn to it. I am quite content to have this one. I think it will keep its value and attractiveness to me for longer that the other glitzy ones. I feel this is the one."*

What does the ring say to that?
"I feel very special. I may not be as big and bold and sexy as the others, but I can give you so much pleasure."

[Scarlet as herself] *"I had to prove that I was all right after I left him. Yes, I needed to say, 'See? I am somebody and I don't need him.' My lifestyle with him would have been flashy. [Pause] You know I didn't realize that dreams were a sort of mirror."*

SCARLET'S THIRD DREAM

In telling me about the next dream, Scarlet told me that she'd tried two ways of working with it. "I went to a website that interprets symbols. It came back with very general things, so I didn't get much from it. When I looked at my dream in the dream-catcher way, it made more sense and I saw it differently. I've also noticed that I don't reach for food now when I'm feeling low. Instead, I ask what I would do if I were really looking after myself. I value myself much more now, and I still haven't dreamt of my ex."

I invited Scarlet to tell me about her dream.

"I am in a speedboat with a very attractive man. The boat is rocking as the waters are very stormy. We are circling the most beautiful island: the waters around it are dark and murky, and so is the sky, but the island itself is bathed in a golden light. I am sitting with my back towards the man and he has his arms around me. I am not scared and I feel (dare I say it?) very beautiful – the ideal James Bond girl. The boat speeds up and we cruise around the island. The stormy skies start to clear and there is sunshine all around.

"The dream then switches to me sitting at a very ornate, seventeenth-century piano with three tiers of keys. The room is also very grand, but there is no other furniture except a very ornate mirror above a huge fireplace and a gold candelabra next to the french windows leading into the garden. The sun is shining into the room, but I am looking at the piano and then the music notes. I cannot read the music and do not understand how to play the instrument or on which keyboard. The main focus is me and the piano."

How did you interpret the dream using the Internet dream dictionary?

"From a general website I picked out several key words to try to help me understand my dream."

These are some of the definitions that Scarlet was offered.

Boat: The boat is a symbol for your life. What kind of waters were you travelling through? Think about how you felt in the dream in order to better understand the message.

Candle: Candles often play a pivotal role in spiritual rituals, and their meaning in your dreams can be just as important. A candle can signify your inner light. It is a sign that you need to look inside yourself and examine what you really want in life and in love. The more aware you are of your true nature, the brighter the flame burns. A burning candle can also indicate an unexpected event, such as a surprise visit or a letter from someone you haven't heard from lately. If you dream of blowing out a candle, it may indicate the end of something significant in your life. Are you about to move or change jobs? Or perhaps it's time to end a certain relationship.

Island: This is an obstacle dream if you were a castaway. The outcome depends on whether you were successful in getting off the island. The dream predicts a new and exciting experience.

Light: Daylight augurs renewed hope. A ray of light signifies the answer to a long-standing problem.

Music: If the music was beautiful, everything in your life will be harmonious. But an irritating cacophony is a sign of discord all around you.

Musical instruments: Dreaming of playing an instrument you don't really know how to play is an omen of a sudden and surprising change in the way you live. A broken instrument is a warning to watch your health. While breaking a string during playing predicts the break-up of a love affair, carrying an instrument forecasts success with members of the opposite sex.

Ocean: The details are important in interpreting a dream that took place on the ocean. If the water was calm, it's a good omen, but choppy waters signify ups and downs. You will need to muster considerable strength of character to ride out the rough waters if you dreamt of a rough or stormy sea. Your action is also a key. An ocean voyage indicates a fortunate respite from your problems. And swimming in the sea is a sign that you are about to widen your sphere of influence.

Piano: Playing the piano is a sign of success for your current plans, but if the piano was out of tune, there will be some delays. Moving a piano forecasts achievement, and tuning one means you'll be hearing good news. To hear a piano beautifully played by another person should be music to your ears when it comes to your financial future.

Storm: This is an obstacle dream. Storms portend a depression that you will get over only when you accept the fact that you are the only one who can really change your life.

Scarlet's dream working.
"I am in the boat with the man and it is very rocky owing to the storm, but I feel very safe and warm and loved as he wraps his arms around me. I am really happy, glowing from within, and I feel so sexy. I have very brown limbs and I'm wearing a white bikini and open white shirt. The troubled waters do not worry me. I feel safe and as we circle the island. I am tantalized and excited by it. I feel this tremendous strength and understanding that this is my paradise and I am travelling the choppy waters to get to it. The island is drawing and inviting me in and I love the thought of the adventure. I feel very calm and relaxed. The storms clear, the water becomes smooth and the boat jets off at high speed, circling the island. I am very excited and stand on the deck feeling very free. The sun is shining and I am glowing and grinning as I know that we are about to land on the island. As I stand alone at the front of the boat, I have the feeling that this is it – this time I am getting closer to my paradise. At the back of the boat my lover is steering. I am very happy.

Scarlet's understanding: *"To me this dream symbolizes that I am circling what I have been searching for all this time – my paradise – but before I reach it, I have to deal with harder times. But I will be all right – safe and loved. I am not alone. I have nothing to fear, yet I must deal with the storm holding me back. My future is out there in front of me and right now I am doing the groundwork to land the boat and live on this island.*

Scarlet's working: *"Sitting in front of the piano I am nervous. I am looking at all three keyboards and then the music, feeling daunted and confused. I keep raising my hands, then pulling them back, too scared to touch a note. I feel muddled and confused, not sure how to understand the music, let alone read it. The music sheet is a whirl of notes that make no sense and seem to go on and on across the sheets.*

"*As the piano. I am very ornate and handsome, having fine ebony and ivory keys. I am a rich walnut wood with an intricate inlaid pattern, well polished. My main bulk (where the strings are kept) is very compact and solid, and my legs are very thin and dainty: there is a certain poise and elegance to me. I have three tiers of keys to play on, and when played well, I have a sweet sound and I'm charming to the ear. However, played badly, I sound squeaky and out of harmony. I am confusing to look at, but pleasing to appreciate and understand.*

Scarlet's understanding: "*I think my playing the piano indicates that I have reached a stage in life when I want to change career. I'm daunted by the choice and not sure which one to pick: should it be the top row of keys, which is easy and accessible, the middle row, or the bottom row, bottom being the hardest to play? I'm not even confident about touching these keys in case I play them out of tune.*

"*I'm not sure how to approach my idea of starting my own business. Should I be working for purely practical reasons (money), or perhaps in some way that uses my insight and understanding? I feel that I have several different levels and could choose any one to make a career, but combining them would be the biggest challenge of all.*

"*It matters not which key is struck as the music will flow and I am there to practise. If at first the music is not flowing, I must practise until it is because the piano will wait for me to hit the right notes. I must be bold and not fear playing a key, no matter how squeaky it is. The music sheet in front of me is a map to follow: although I cannot read it, I must trust my instinct and learn to listen to the message in the music.*"

Judith

An attractive but self-deprecating young woman from a restrictive Northern Irish background, Judith had the dream about starving cows in Chapter 5. Her parents were ambitious for her and in order to protect her from the local teenage boys, they sent her away for a convent education. She grew up making perfectionist demands of herself to please and be pleasing, remnants of which continue to operate to this day not only in her work but also in her private life. Judith's social life has improved a great deal, and although she is getting a lot more recognition at work (she is a valued staff member at a hospice), she feels that she has "done her time" and would now like to work in an environment more nurturing for her. She enjoys life, and although some of her damaging patterns persist, she has given herself much more freedom and has an altogether better opinion of herself. She is no longer willing to be a dogsbody. She values her dream wisdom and through it has gained the confidence to present the following dream.

JUDITH'S FIRST DREAM

"I'm in my flat with a mother and baby. In my kitchen I go to open the bin and it's a quarter full of shit; it's human shit and I am absolutely aghast. I have no idea where it's come from. It seems to have been there for a while, and I'm thinking how has it got here? Has the mother who's been looking after the child put it there? And why hasn't it been put it in the toilet? I'm really caught up with why it's in my bin."

Be the shit. We don't know what shit is, so describe it.
"Well, er…I'm a waste product from humans. When they finish digesting their food, they expel what they don't want. So I'm a waste product."
(She sounds distressed, which is how she's been feeling lately – that she is no longer wanted in a relationship and has been expelled.)

Tell us your experience in the dream.
"My experience as shit in the dream? I'm in Judith's bin in her kitchen in her flat. I'm in a grey bin and I'm old and dried up." [Chokes a bit as she recognizes her fear of being abandoned and becoming old and dried up.]

So as this shit, you've been there for some time?
"Yes. Something that goes through my head is, 'Who's taken this old shit and put it in my bin?' because it looks like old shit."

Well, let's ask the shit how it got there.
[Laughing] *"Someone had to put me in there."*

Just say that again: "Someone had to put me in this place."
(The dream-catcher asks for this repetition so that Judith will realize that her difficulties are not all her own fault.)

"Someone had to put me in this place." [Sounds relieved and nods thoughtfully]

Well, how are we going to find out?
"We could ask the people who are there. I'll ask the mother. I don't know who she is."

Be her.
"I'm somebody who has come to visit Judith. I'm staying with her for a while and it's nice for me and my child." [Admits to feeling tearful as she says this]

What's there to be tearful about?
"Having someone to stay with me is something I enjoy, and the woman who is staying with me in the dream also seems to enjoy being with me." (Judith begins to realize that she might not have to remain alone. Perhaps there is some part of herself that is likeable, and someone in reality might enjoy staying with her.)

We don't know what a mother is. Are you young?
"I'm a young woman. I think I am a single mother actually and I've got a child and my purpose as a mother is to look after the child and to make sure that I meet my child's needs. In the dream I'm playing with the child, or at least taken up with the child while Judith is looking in the bin. [Laughs as she recognizes how often she is caught up with looking at rejection and disappointment]

Judith's coming to ask you about this old shit that's in the bin. Do you know anything about it?
"No. I was immediately going to say that it doesn't belong to me. It doesn't belong to us; we wouldn't have done that to you." [Quiet tears – silence as she takes in what she has said]

(This identifying with and speaking out as a character in the dream enables Judith to hear and affirm that she does not deserve to be treated badly. This sort of confirmation is much more valuable than any outside reassurance can be. Judith is now starting to emerge from the self-hatred that is often felt after a rejection.)

You had this dream last night?
"No, about a week ago."
(This timing is significant, since the previous day Judith had confronted the difficulty she was having with a friend. Instead of storing it away and hoarding her "shit", she had cleared up the issue. Her dreaming had already laid the foundation for a change in her behaviour, even before she unwrapped her dream.)

Be the bin, please.
"I'm a grey plastic, common [laughs] *domestic kitchen bin.* [Grinning] *I'm one of millions. There's nothing very special about me. I'm just a grey plastic bin in Judith's kitchen. I'm small, not too tall and I've got a pedal and a cover, and I am a quarter full of shit."*

Say that again.
"I'm a quarter full of shit." [Speaking more passionately now]

(Asking for a repetition when a dreamer's voice drops or there is struggle for words may enable them to hear themselves more clearly. We school ourselves to skip over and avoid uncomfortable feelings that are unacceptable or too difficult to face. Repeating gives more time to feel what a dream is drawing our attention to. You can do a version of this for yourself. If a sentence or phrase jumps out at you while recording your dream, explore it further by repeating it aloud for yourself.)

"This shit belongs in the toilet. It belongs in some place where it can be safely disposed of and treated. I am not here to have shit dumped in me. I deal with waste, but not this type of waste. This is kind of toxic and I remember that when Judith saw this shit in me, she became upset because she felt that it would contaminate the child." [Silence and tears as she realizes how deeply she has rejected and punished herself]

You're connecting here?

[Judith as herself] *"I've been a bit worried about whether I have enough to offer a child if I ever had one."*

Worrying that the shit in you might contaminate your child?
"Yes." [Long silence]

Well, you have this dilemma in your dream. What are you going to do about it? (Here the dream-catcher is inviting Judith to use her ability to free-associate, to take the opportunity to work creatively on this part of the dream.)

"The shit needs to go in the toilet. I feel ashamed of it actually – ashamed of this amount of shit in the bin. How the hell has it got there? I'm really preoccupied with that."
(Judith is often preoccupied with something it would be better to let go of.)

Yes, do that. Put it down the toilet.
"OK… It takes some time to go down because there's quite a bit of it, but I'm flushing it. I really think it's appalling, this amount of shit."

But you can get rid of it? You can flush it away?
[Powerfully] *"I'm determined it's going. I just have to use the flushing mechanism a lot and stay by it."*

(All the group laugh as they identify with this symbolism and its real-life implications: the need to stick with difficulties until they are flushed out.)

What's a flushing mechanism?
"Something complicated. It's a pump that has a lever. You have to push a lever that releases water from one container into another. Flushing water takes things away and down the system."

What would that be in a human system?
(Here the dream-catcher invites Judith to make the connection between her fantasy work and what it may symbolize in real life.)
"Tears – yes, it would be tears flushing away. Oh, dear. [Quietly tearful again] So many tears."

All that sadness.

"Yes, and after all that flushing I'd feel nice and clean as the bin, but I don't think I'd want to take it back into the kitchen just yet. It needs some air."

(Here Judith describes the natural experience of needing space to herself after owning her hurt and allowing her tears.)

So it's possible to deal with this toxic waste. Don't get hung up on who put it there. It might take years to find out. What you need to do is just what you're doing – flush it away. Trust your thought. This is your dream and you will know when you've finished working on it. What more do you want?

"I can start again and I don't have to worry. The shit's going and it won't contaminate anybody."

Any advice for yourself?

[Firmly] *"The first thing I've got to say is that I'm really glad you've dumped the shit. At least you've got some relief – you don't have to go about in an appalling state."*

What do you suggest now? How are you going to help this woman?

"Well, my first thought is that I need to take more support. My first thought was, 'You need to see a doctor.' My second thought was, 'No! You need a friend.' [Laughs in a hearty, open way] *That's it really.* [Confirming to herself now] *That's it! I don't need to treat myself so badly. I was distressed and didn't know where to put myself, and rather than lay it on someone, I held on to it."*

At home that night Judith wrote down some thoughts that had been clarified by the dream-working session:

"Someone who hoards shit (feelings and thoughts no longer appropriate or useful) is not able to let go of waste (the feeling that all is lost). They make precious what is no longer useful or worth attention. Shitty thought assumes great importance in their lives, little else has any meaning. They abandon themselves to what has been wasted. Often it is all they've got. Lose that and they believe there is nothing.

"I hold on to shitty toxic thoughts and feelings rather than let go and face my grief and sadness. I recycle old, shitty material rather than flush it out of my life. A few months back, I lost a grip of myself. I abandoned myself to shit rather than clean up my act [a reference to a complicated relationship with a girlfriend she had felt hurt and rejected by]. My need for hoarding shitty thoughts had to be acknowledged before I could move on. Once I honoured my distress and opened to my grief, my 'shit' could be dumped. I now have more room for nourishment in my life."

Ivor

Ivor was a member of a gestalt training group. At the start of his training, his interchanges habitually took the form of either offering or gathering pieces of information. He seemed to be the group monitor. He was eager to know and do it right. He was always asking questions and showed little confidence in his own experience and the value of his internal knowing. He offered his cleverness rather than himself. Although his fellow trainees were fond of him, they often disregarded what he said. They wanted him, a real person, not an encyclopedia. A turning-point in his training came when he had the following dream.

IVOR'S DREAM
"I am at some sort of fair. At the fair I am in front of a bookstall. There are no books on the table; they are all on the ground underneath the stall. Among the books I see one called The History of Latvia. *It is large and obviously a book of quality. It looks very bright compared to the remainder of the stock, with a stand-out, creamy-coloured cover. As well as the volume looking attractive the subject interests me (my paternal grandfather was born in Lithuania, and I have discovered that the village he was born in is now in Latvia). I want to buy the book but it's not that straightforward. I must go through a ritual of firing three darts at it in order to secure it."*

Be the book.
"I am The History of Latvia. *I am a collection of pages bound together. I have a lot of information in me about the past. I have an attractive cover and I am nicely bound to keep my pages neatly together,*

otherwise I would spill all over the place and some of my pages would get lost."

[Ivor as himself] *"I forget exactly how much I know, partly because the information is hidden in my memory and partly because I take what I know for granted until someone else draws my attention to it. I also tend to overlook that my past is very with me. I have an olive complexion, so some of my Russo-Jewish inheritance shows."*

Where are you now book?
"Now I am being sold cheaply. I'm dumped under this table where no one can really see me. And my owner has said that if anyone wants to buy me, I must be pierced by three darts. However, Ivor finds me among all the books the stallholder has put under the table."

Notice what you say?
(In real life Ivor is a secondhand bookseller and he habitually sells himself cheaply. He has resisted making a career, perhaps because he needed to resist his parents' longing for him to "make something of himself". His choice had been to make do by selling secondhand books, even though this means he has to live cheaply and is constantly short of money. Making do is, of course, part of his heritage; his parents also survived on very little throughout the war and during their early days in the UK.)

Now be the stall-owner.
[Standing up] *"The stallholder no longer seems interested in selling the books; he is moving on. He is not even displaying his wares; he is hiding them under a table. The customer really has to work for the goods, seek them out and undergo extraordinary feats in order to win them."*
(Ivor is standing because actively being the people and things in a dream can help the dreamer to identify more closely. His words reflect how he must have felt during his childhood – never good enough, a common feeling among immigrants trying to fit into a strange country.)

Stallholder, what is your purpose?
"I no longer want to sell books. I'm no longer interested in history.

I have better things to do now and you can take the books with the test, or leave them."

[Ivor as himself] *"All this leads me to the idea that I am also letting go of some of my past."*

Ivor said that his parents had hidden their cultural heritage. He was choked and tearful here, and talked about how he felt at having the door closed on his past. He made links with how he now wouldn't/couldn't let go of his parents. This also connected with how he felt that he was never good enough for them, when perhaps they were afraid of not being good enough themselves. All this evoked in Ivor was a familiar feeling of something missing – that his parents were holding out on him in some way, which made it difficult for him to leave them. Becoming a secondhand bookseller seemed to be linked in some way to his dilemma: perhaps books/history being more important than money?

Ivor "became" the book full of his history and culture. We who witnessed him were very moved as he confronted the bookseller about undervaluing the book's worth by keeping it under the table. We could hear echoes of his struggle with his parents, and invited Ivor to talk with them now as the book, and show them how substantial he was. He told them he was a record of all his history and theirs. He said if they cut him out of their lives, they would be the poorer.

Through being the book, Ivor realized that he no longer needed his parents to validate him. Rather than focusing on what he felt they had denied him, he looked at what they had given him. He opened his heart and released them from any obligation to him.

What is it you need now?
"I suppose I need to say goodbye to my parents. [Pause] Mum and Dad, I need to say goodbye to you. I'm grateful for your having brought me up. I will still come and see you, but I have to leave you so as to make my own way. [Weeping] This is a big thought. I have held on to the belief that there is no choice – that how I am is decided by fate, that I couldn't help it. Now this choosing one's path is a very different attitude."

Recalling the work later, Ivor said: "The leave-taking in that dream-work was part of my growing away from my parents and into myself. This dream had its part to play in helping me complete my training and even in taking me through some of the stages that followed, such as passing my assessment and taking on my first clients. Perhaps this dream-work was connected to meeting those subsequent stages in an adult way. While I was tied to my parents, I was liable to be dismissive of adulthood in a 'Who, me?' way."

This dream provided an important piece of Ivor's puzzle. Up to this point he had made some progress, but seemed too often to yo-yo back into his old, ineffectual position. He was not often taken seriously by others, and would play the joker to make a place for himself. He seemed unable to grow fully into his life. Now he started to take his place in the training group differently, using his skills and talents with more authority. He gained respect rather than sympathy from the other group members, who were delighted to see him empower himself in this way. He had given up trying to collect this indefinable debt. He decided to go it alone.

Talking later about his experience of dream-catching, he said: "I find that when I am being an item in the dream, I am concentrating on the process of describing: it is only after I hear what I have said as a self-description that I know what I've said. I don't do the two simultaneously; I doubt if I could."

(This is one reason why a dream-catcher may ask the dreamer to repeat and hear for themselves what it is that they are saying.) ✩

7

CATCHING
YOUR DREAM

"To take the copy not as a copy
but as reality itself."

PLATO (C. 427–347 BC)

D reams belong to you, the dreamer. They are symbolic creations whose meaning only you can unravel. You are the dream. Each role or object of the dream is a projection of you, each symbol playing a part in working out your life script. Even familiar people, places and things in your dreams represent aspects of you. They are clues to help you understand the different possibilities being offered through your dreaming.

This chapter outlines some structures and forms that can be used to get the most out of your dreams. It will show you how to keep a dream journal, compile your own personal dream dictionary and improve your dream recall.

Remembering your dreams

Some people find it difficult to remember their dreams. This isn't surprising since research has shown that the area of the brain associated with memory is closed down during sleep. No wonder dreams seem so elusive: we can catch them only as we are emerging from sleep. Even people who remember dreams easily can access them only just before waking. The other three or four dreaming periods that occur during the night are lost – unless you programme yourself to wake as soon as a dream starts.

There are reports of people instructing their subconscious to wake them when dreaming and then suffering sleepless nights as they surf their dreams. Others have set alarm clocks to wake them several times during the night in order to catch their dreams, usually successfully. Only the truly dedicated fish for dreams in these ways. Most of us find it sufficient to write them down as soon as we wake, before there is time to be distracted and forget them.

Some people have developed elaborate rituals in order to get themselves into the right frame of mind to receive their dreams. Dream Catchers tends to favour trying the simplest method first. If that doesn't work, then increase your efforts until you are successful. You can train yourself to remember your dreams in the same way as you can instruct yourself to wake up at a certain hour. Just say three times before you sleep, "I will remember my dreams." When you first wake up, lie still and recall them; you need only a snippet. Move very slowly and write the dream down in the present, as if it's happening now. It may take a week to catch a dream, but be patient – it usually works.

If after a week you are still struggling to catch a dream, you might need to use some of the hints that follow.

Hints for helping dream recall

- A warm milky drink at bedtime can help lull you into a relaxed state conducive to dreaming.
- Clear your head by thinking back on the day that has just passed. Pay attention to its positive aspects, note any worries you might have and give them to your unconscious to sort out for you.
- Avoid drinking alcohol or taking any form of drug before sleeping as it might inhibit your dreaming.
- Thumb through your dream journal (if you have started one) and think about other dreams you have had.
- Ask your unconscious for a dream. Think about an issue that you would like resolved and ask for a dream about it. Repeat to yourself several times, "I would like a dream about..."
- Try to empty your mind of the day's worries by doing the following relaxation exercise:

  1 Lie back, close your eyes and breathe in and out slowly and deeply for a couple of minutes. Allow your breath to leave your body fully before you inhale again.

  2 Breathe in and tense your feet, relaxing them as you breathe out. Do the same with your calf muscles, then your thighs, abdomen and so on until you reach your head and every part of your body has been separately relaxed. Let your weight sink into the bed.

  3 When you feel completely relaxed, tell yourself that you would like a dream and that you will remember it.

  4 Picture yourself gently waking up in the morning and recording your dream in your journal. Rehearse this visualization until you fall asleep.

- Set your alarm for slightly earlier than usual. When you wake, lie quietly, keeping totally still, as the mind begins erasing dreams the moment you start moving.

- Keeping your eyes closed, your first thought should be: "What was I just dreaming?" Don't think about the coming day. Recall your dream and try to work backwards through it in your mind, gathering as many details as you can. If you remember a scene, ask yourself what happened before it. If you find yourself falling asleep again while doing this, go straight to writing down your dream.
- Reach for your dream journal and write out your dream as if it is happening in the present, for example: "I am walking along a narrow path." Don't delay, or important dreams may be lost.

Improving your dream recall

It is not known why some people can remember their dreams in detail, while others remember nothing at all. However, it is known that everybody dreams several times each night and that there are ways of improving your ability to remember dreams. As with any other skill, practice is essential to make significant progress. Don't worry if you miss a dream. If its underlying theme is important, it will occur again, perhaps in a different form. Once you start paying attention to your dreams, they will begin to surface more readily, and you should notice a dramatic improvement within a month. But if you still cannot remember dreams, it might be that your unconscious is withholding them. See Chapter 9 for information on what to do about this.

Dream journals

While it is possible to work on dreams without keeping written accounts, a well-kept dream journal is a powerful reference tool, providing a fascinating record of your personal milestones. It will connect you strongly to your dreams, improving your power of recall as well as your dream-catching skill.

When you are just starting out, it is worth noting down everything you can remember from each dream, no matter how fragmentary. Even the smallest snippets can be used as starting points for exploring a dream. Sometimes just jotting down objects, colours, places or feelings can help you remember more. As you become more skilful, you will instinctively know which dreams have special significance for you and perhaps those will be the only ones you choose to record. Eventually, you might even begin to understand your dream's messages as you are writing them down.

Looking through your dream journals years later will give you a vivid reminder of events long forgotten. You will be able to see the changes in your circumstances and the evolution of your consciousness over the passage of time. There will be links with previous dreams, and you will recognize the patterns and symbols of your ongoing life themes. Mapping these connections and changes will give you a fascinating insight into how you are progressing with your existential tasks. In addition, many dreamers are delighted and amazed at the level of creativity their journals hold. Some have even used the stuff of their dreams as the basis of novels.

SELECTING A JOURNAL

Choose a beautiful book containing paper that you will enjoy writing and drawing on. Even if you don't consider yourself artistic, you might be inspired by the images that come to you in dreams. Capture them – sketch them or paint them – they will make a vibrant record of your internal journeys.

Within a well-planned dream journal you can organize a special place to jot down your inspirational thinking as it occurs to you. Perhaps leave a few lines' space after each dream account so that you can record your insights and note their significance. Ideally, give yourself lots of space to experiment with different layouts and to find a way of recording that gives you pleasure.

Persist with your dream journal. At first it may contain just snatches of dreams, but as your memory and dream-catching skills improve, it is sure to develop in richness and insight, providing you with a treasure trove of personal wisdom. Your dream journal is a record of your innermost thoughts and feelings, so keep it in a safe place.

Useful journal-keeping tips
- Record your dreams all together and in sequence.
- Keep your journal and a pen within easy reach of your bedside; getting up to hunt for them will almost certainly limit what you are able to remember.

- Put the date at the top of a clean page before you go to sleep, and use a bookmark so that you can find your place easily.
- Write as fluently as possible, and don't worry about your handwriting, spelling or the actual order of events. Record everything that you can think of: people, places colours, smells, emotions. It doesn't matter if it seems to make no sense: you just need an authentic account of what happened and how you felt.
- Make a special note of any image that stood out.
- Whether you are artistically inclined or not, make a sketch or comic strip of your dream.
- If you are in a hurry to get up, jot your dream down in note form. These "headlines" might give you enough prompts to work through later.
- Read your dream over and note down what you think and feel it about it. Trust your associations. Make a note of any major concerns you are dealing with at present.
- Ask your dream what its message is.
- Give your dream a title – whatever first occurs to you.

Dream themes

Some people can recall several dreams a night, which almost invariably are linked by a common theme that might not emerge until all the dreams are worked through. It's as if the subconscious is trying out different ways of looking at the same issue. Often the dreams will show a progression, moving towards a solution, with the last dream clearly consolidating the message. Progression is also evident in dreams that occur over longer periods of time. When you are able to recognize your dreams' themes, you will have reached a point where you do not have to work out each dream thoroughly. You will be able to see at a glance what they are about, recognizing familiar themes and symbols as short-hand versions of your dream's message.

Nightmares and recurring dreams should be recorded in exactly the same way as other dreams. If you are processing your dreams regularly, your journal will show you how they have been building up, and this alone could help reduce their frequency. At Dream Catchers we have never yet worked through a nightmare that has not had a positive outcome.

Your personal dream dictionary

At some time or other most people try using a dream dictionary to decipher their dreams. Many find it an unsatisfactory experience simply because there are numerous symbols in a dream and you often end up with a disjointed patchwork of information which can leave you more confused than when you started (see Scarlet's efforts in Chapter 6). Put bluntly, commercial dictionaries are inadequate because they work on the premise that symbols have the same meaning for everybody. They cannot encompass the originality, creativity and purpose of our individual dreaming process.

While some symbols permit generalization (water, for example, signifying an emotional or spiritual issue), their specific significance to an individual's life can only truly be recognized by the dreamer. Is the water a rough sea, a sluggish river, a babbling brook? What does each signify, and in what context? Only the dreamer can tell. By identifying with individual parts of your dreams you can discover your own meanings and start to compile a useful glossary of symbols and characters that have importance in your dream world. These symbols are the only ones that will have any real and constant significance for you, and even they will change over time. Recognizing your own dream language provides a short cut to finding the essential messages within your dreams.

Make an alphabetical list of your dream symbols and have fun noting down the definitions. You will then have a ready source of reference to help your future dream-work. Remember that the same characters, locations and symbols can crop up in all sorts of dreams, so make sure you update your dream dictionary regularly. Your dream symbols can serve as a reminder or a warning when you are in (or heading for) a situation similar to one you have already experienced. Paying attention to particular types of dream or dream symbol could alert you to potentially harmful issues and thus enable you to avoid serious problems.

> **Cataloguing dream symbols**
> - Any time you encounter a particularly powerful character or animal in a dream, note it down. It will almost certainly be central to your working through of that particular dream.
> - Once you have identified with it, write down what it represented for you. You will then begin to notice each time that symbol or character recurs.
> - Note any variations in the appearance of symbols. For example, a tabby cat might later appear in a different colour or size, while a character could behave in a completely different manner.
> - Allow enough space after each entry to record future changes of the symbol.
> - When you've gathered several different dreams in your journal, go through them and note any symbols that recur. Look back to what their significance has been and see if there are any links between them and the types of issues that you were dealing with at that time, such as career moves, new relationships or pregnancy.

Your dream dictionary is not intended to replace the dream-catching process, because each dream has particular significance for the time it was dreamt. Your symbols will continue to evolve as your consciousness expands. Your catalogue of symbols will be a valuable short-hand guide, but nothing is fixed, and the changes you notice will be fascinating.

Dream-sharing

Once you have caught some dreams for yourself, you will probably feel the urge to share them with others. A word of caution here: your dreams are not always as interesting to others as they are to you. Select your moment, tell your dream story briefly and you could inspire a dream novice to start taking notice of their own dreams.

Some cultures incorporate dream-sharing into their daily activities. Perhaps the most well known are the Senoi of Malaysia, for whom dream-sharing sets the day's agenda. They regard the study of dreams as a vital part of every child's education.

No matter how willing you are to learn from your dreams, you may unconsciously censor them by skipping over apparently unimportant parts, or forgetting details as you go along. In order to benefit fully from dream-catching it is useful to have access to a dream-catching partner. They will observe your tone of voice and body language – things that might habitually be outside your awareness.

Regular contact with members of a dream group can also prove invaluable. When weekend and residential training groups share their dreams during morning sessions, participants get a good idea of what the issues and difficulties of the day are going to be. Getting to know other people's dreams and how they relate to their symbols will facilitate your own dream-catching skills. You will gain in confidence and, perhaps most importantly, you will benefit from other perspectives. You will feel entertained, moved and privileged to watch others growing through their dreams. ☆

8

DIFFICULT
DREAMS

"Learn from your dreams what you lack."

W.H. Auden (1907–73)

B ible stories, literature and films have all used dreams to illustrate distress or mental disturbance. However, few people realize that each "bad" dream holds within it a healing potential for the dreamer. Once worked through, nightmares lose their power to make us afraid. Even the most violent and terrifying of dreams contain keys to the well-being of the dreamer.

A young anorexic woman had a horrific dream about being chased at night through the countryside by an unknown man. As she ran, her legs became leaden and she could hear him gaining on her, even feel his breath on her neck. She stumbled and fell, then woke up. She was very afraid during the telling of the dream and was most reluctant to look at it further. She could identify only with herself in the dream and said that in real life she too felt very afraid, exhausted and pursued.

Eventually, her curiosity about her pursuer led her to imagine turning around and facing him. When, in waking fantasy, she imagined herself doing this, she was surprised to see that he also stopped running. She asked him why he was chasing her and he said he thought something was wrong with her and was following to see if he could help. She laughed at this, agreed that there was something wrong with her and that she was difficult to help as she was constantly running away because of her fear of being trapped.

Like many sufferers of anorexia, she was unable to keep still, constantly moving in order to burn calories, even though she denied to herself that this behaviour, along with starvation, could hasten her death. Now, perhaps for the first time, she acknowledged that she was a danger to herself. She could see, through identifying with the man in her dream, that part of her was concerned for her welfare – a part that wanted to stop running and ask for help.

Dreams are similar to the fairy tales of childhood in that they magnify our predicaments and starkly represent our conflicts. Having the courage to see the value of our darker side can start a healing process.

Dealing with fear and aggression

Many of us learned in childhood that aggressive or sexual feelings were bad, and now we live in an uneasy truce with our primitive instincts, not knowing that negative feelings have an essential defensive function in our lives. Those of us who have been rigidly controlled as children may ourselves become rigidly controlling. In dreams, however, behaviours that we have learned to suppress gain their freedom, and forbidden desires and emotions push for acknowledgement. Feelings writ large in our dreams offer us some emotional release during sleep. They also alert us to issues that need our attention.

Aggression is an essential part of our life force. Healthy aggression enables us to reach out for what we need, "go for it" when we must, and stand our ground when we have to. Unfortunately, because we are so afraid of our negative feelings our attempts to hold back socially unacceptable behaviour may also cause us to supress healthy agression and passion. Denying the darker sides of our nature can lead to dire consequences for us personally and for society. If we cannot admit to negative feelings, we will almost inevitably project them on to other individuals, races or nations, which can lead to tragedy. Pointing the finger at negative attributes in others is usually in the service of denying them in ourselves.

Aggression turns sour only when it is inhibited and suppressed. Then it may fuel hostility or even turn inwards, manifesting itself as depression or psychosomatic illness. Maturity, experience and learning to respect and use our darker nature positively may eventually enable us to transform our frustrations into something other than abuse, irritation or rage. Our dreams invite us to make this transformation. When we flee from out shadow we invite persecution.

Jung urged us to unlock our vitality through facing and owning our shadow. Freud, on the other hand, suggested that the energy held within our forbidden thoughts, feelings and desires should be translated into creative activities. He believed that this process, which he called sublimation, distinguished man from beast. The sublime creations of angst-ridden artists and the cut-throat exertions of the executive squash player both give credence to this way of thinking.

Unexpressed feelings do not go away – they remain in storage, frequently tumbling out at inappropriate moments. The strain of holding back can make us hyper-sensitive to slights, injustices or misunderstandings, and insignificant incidents may become exaggerated out of all proportion. Emotional energy will always push for discharge and is frequently vented on those less powerful than ourselves. This "pecking order" aggression is graphically demonstrated in the animal world. Helen has noticed that if she scolds her dogs, the more dominant of the two immediately vents his aggression on the other animal.

Human beings can respond in a similar way. When we do not receive the respect or attention we deserve, we may be left with vengeful feelings. Most of us have experienced an urge for Old Testament-style vengeance in order to pass on a hurt and reassert our power. In the absence of the original culprit, we simply impose our will on those around us.

A VENGEFUL CUT

Single and used to being independent, Angela found herself feeling trapped and frustrated in a relationship with Tom, a man who seemed to need constant control of all their activities. The final straw for her came when he drew a line down the middle of a piece of Brie she had bought for them both as a treat out of her own money: he was afraid that she would eat more than her fair share.

Feeling beside herself with rage, Angela decided to spend the weekend in Edinburgh with a close male friend. She was conscious that doing so would probably end her relationship with Tom, but she could not face the interminable discussions that other ways of extricating herself would involve. On her return, she found Tom distraught, angry and uncommunicative, refusing either to talk to her or leave her house. Angela went to her room, exhausted and emotionally fatigued, and fell asleep, only to wake with an image of cutting off Tom's genitals. She was shocked. She had never seen herself as a ball-breaker. She had always liked men better than women, and to own this image was devastating for her. She rushed to a friend for support and asked for help in working on the dream. She knew she was angry with her lover, but found the image of castrating him unacceptable.

Identifying with the severed genitals in the dream, she said:
"When connected and used well, I am an organ of procreation and sexual pleasure. However, I can withhold and withdraw, and now I am completely useless as I have been cut off in anger."

This enabled her to see how castrating her rage really was. She recognized that she had also cut off her own power and pleasure in the relationship by constantly compromising and trying to make it work. By being so self-defeatingly reasonable for so long, the pressure had built up until she had finally cut and run.

In some cases, the greater our capacity to store up emotions, the bigger the time-bomb we are walking around with. The feelings evoked by abandonment and betrayal may seem to be forgotten, until they are triggered into passionate outpourings months or even years later. Stories about mild-mannered men committing frenzied murder are legion.

Angela was now faced with the fact that her reasonableness and compromise had covered an immense frustration, culminating in a deeply angry act of withdrawal. Somewhere along the line, Tom had sensed her anger and drawing away from him, but his response had been to become even more insecure and controlling. The relationship was over and had been for some time, but neither of them had had the courage to face it.

After working on the image from her dream, Angela also realized that her profound fear and loathing of men. It seemed that she had reached a bottom line and only now could she truly work towards healing the wounds that had caused such hatred in her in the first place.

When unconscious memories are suddenly reactivated by a current hurt or injustice, our dreams may leave us struggling with feelings that echo from childhood. Links to our past experiences are often hidden, so we may be unable to make sense of our waking disquiet. Sometimes these traces of feeling are so slight that a dreamer may experience only a vague sense of foreboding or powerlessness.

FAMILY SECRETS

Denise, a wife, mother and professional woman, brought Helen this dream.
"I am at home (but it is different from home) with my sister. We are in an upstairs room collaborating together and we are waiting for our father to knock on the door. We are collaborating about the questions that we want to ask him. There is a sense of us working together and I am keeping close to her. Then there is a knock on the door and it's my Uncle Gordon. He comes in and starts taking over, telling us what to do, and then I wake up. My father never does knock on the door."

Say that again.
"My father never does knock on the door." [Looks sad]

Tell your father that you are waiting for him to knock on the door.
[Full of feeling] *"I am waiting for you to knock on the door, but you never have. There are so many questions that I need to ask you. You left and didn't come back to see me, even after mother died. You effectively made me an orphan. [Tearful] It must be even worse for my sister, she must have thought it was her fault."*

(She had always had a rather tense relationship with her sister, who was "difficult" and did not have a cheerful disposition.)

Denise then recounted how her father had left after a note written by her sister was found, alleging that he had indecently propositioned her. After this, her sister was taken away to live with her grandparents and her father vanished for ever. Nothing more was said about the matter. Her mother seemed never to recover from her heartbreak and died a few years later.

How was that for you, having both your father and your sister disappear?
[Tearfully] *"I didn't understand it. I don't really know what happened and my sister and I don't talk about it now, although that is really because I don't want to know... That's probably why I called it "collaborating" – it's all so secret... It must have been awful for her. No wonder she's so difficult and spiky."*

And how did you cope with this?
"I kept quiet."

You must have thought something was dreadfully wrong – that people could just disappear, be sent away, if they did something wrong.
"I don't remember feeling that. Except I do remember that I couldn't stay at nursery school – I was just so distressed. And every time I was left at my grandparents' house, even though I never made a fuss, I was panicking and screaming inside. Starting school was terrible: I was so frightened and distraught." [Weeps]

Each time they left you, you must have been afraid that they would never take you back.
[Nods through her tears] *"This now makes sense of why my sister is so against me getting an au pair: she must be afraid that we are cutting her off from Sophie* [Denise's four-year-old daughter] *just as she was cut off from me when I was little. Poor thing – I feel so sorry for her. It wasn't her fault...it was his."*

What do you want to say to him?
"All this was your fault! You have ruined our family. You have caused so

much pain. No wonder you didn't come back – how could you face us? You ruined my life. You have ruined us all. My poor sister..."

Can you tell her this?

[To her sister] *"I am so sorry. Now we're in this together."*

[To Helen] *"This experience fits with me and Sophie. No wonder I'm so over-protective and can't bear to leave her. I hate the thought of her first day at school. I'm so afraid that she will feel abandoned."*

You give her the understanding and protection you didn't have?

"Yes. This work is for her as well as me, so I can stop over-protecting her."

What about Uncle Gordon?

[As uncle] *"Oh, harrumph, harrumph! Do this. This is the way – it should be done like this. Organize! Organize!"*

What are you doing in the dream, Uncle Gordon?

"I'm telling them they shouldn't wait for their father. I'm sorting everything out. I'm protecting them."

[Denise as herself] *"He's so overbearing, organizing, controlling and out of touch – even now. He doesn't see that we are grown up and can look after ourselves. This is just how he still is. Little Sophie can't understand him."*

And what about this organizing, harrumphing part of you?

"Yes, I'm like that too, especially when I get panicked about protecting Sophie from feeling abandoned. I rush around trying to sort everything out. Oh! I suppose that's the part of me that feels so responsible for everyone. [Pause] You know, this all makes sense. It seems I have always felt unsafe, insecure. It's only since I've been with Vince that I've felt safe. I know he won't abandon me. He's older than me, and I've thought about that quite a lot. It's not that I see him as a dad. I just want to be young. It seems that I grew up so careful and good. I grew up too fast. Vince is great because he likes to look after me and there's nothing of me that he rejects... [Thoughtful silence] Gosh! This goes right to

the centre of me. I feel sort of...whole. [Laughs] *I was going to say wholesome. I feel as if I have some ground under my feet, even though my legs are propped up on a stool. I feel grounded."*

Experience has taught us to avoid certain situations, to suppress certain feelings. Psychotherapists recognize that in many cases what we are most afraid of has already happened. These fears are based on previous experiences – the things that happened when we were powerless children, or victims of circumstances beyond our control. How would this be for you? To know that what you most fear has already happened and that you have survived it? That the anxiety you feel could be the unexpressed feelings of years ago pushing for release?

Most people have no idea that their dreams are valiantly working away trying to clear the backlog of their unfinished business and unexpressed feelings. Many of us are so habitually numbed we no longer even recognize that we are angry or hurt. We manage to live walled up within our defence systems, maintaining a minimum of contact in the hope of provoking a minimum of pain. The *I Ching* has something to say about life-restricting limitations: "If a man should seek to impose galling limitations upon his own nature, it would be injurious. And if he should go too far in imposing limitations on others, they would seek to rebel. Therefore it is necessary to set limits even upon limitation."

We all need to have our feelings recognized and accepted for what they are. Feelings are energetic, physical phenomena often described in active terms – shaking with fear, moved to tears, hot with anger... It takes a lot of energy to hold back emotions – many of us have experienced punishment or rejection when showing our true feelings and therefore seek refuge in secretiveness and isolation. We have become afraid of our feelings and cynical about the possibility of being accepted. Yet acceptance is what we most long for.

When misunderstandings arise we may retreat before they have been cleared up. Then hurt piles upon hurt and internalized rage may turn into suicidal depression. Immersion in religion, loud music, alcohol or drugs might help to numb our pain, but they rarely support us to make the changes we need to make. Usually, it is only when a crisis erupts or we yearn for more to our lives that we take the courage to look within ourselves. Much distress could be avoided if we regularly listened to our dreams and tended to our needs.

Understanding our dreams brings a new consciousness and invites us to become responsible for our actions. Dreams can also provide inspiration and give us permission to act on our inner knowing, which too often is whittled away away or dulled by socialization and conditioning.

A dream is a concentrated experience. For centuries, mystics have recognized the power and usefulness of dreams. We learn life's lessons slowly – our understanding and insights are gathered painstakingly by taking responsibility for our own mistakes and forgiving those of others. If we are fortunate we will find the support of good teachers. Our dreams, on the other hand, seem to accelerate our experiences, condensing them into intense episodes full of feeling that when deciphered may yield important insights.

The relief felt by dreamers when they access and make sense of their feelings via dreams is physically apparent. Their expression becomes open, their posture is uplifted and they reach out to others. They face the future with optimism.

Recurring dreams

Every recurring dream, whether trivial or gut-joltingly uncomfortable, has a useful message: part of our life requires attention, but what is it? Apart from a nagging disquiet, we may have no conscious idea of how the dream connects to our everyday activities. Only through deciphering its cryptic form can we fully understand its message. When a dreamer begins to understand and action the message within a recurring dream, the dream will start to change, and eventually fade, returning only if difficulties of a similar nature reappear.

FAT FREE-RANGE GUINEA PIGS

Kathy said that every so often she would dream about her childhood pets (rabbits and guinea-pigs). In her dreams they were often in a terrible state, forgotten and neglected. She described them as bright, energetic and friendly animals that needed proper food and loving care in a clean environment. When asked how she was like this, she said that for quite a while she had felt trapped in the cage of her busy schedule and had been neglecting her diet; she certainly hadn't been getting enough attention or cuddles. She got in touch with how resentful she felt that no one was looking after her, then resolved to start giving herself more of what she needed. Gradually, her dreams started changing and the condition of her animals improved. Occasionally they would appear neglected again, and she knew she needed to look after herself better. Eventually she was dreaming of fat, free-range guinea-pigs.

At a later date, Kathy dreamt that her pet rabbit had escaped and was happily nibbling grass on the verge of a very busy road. In the dream she rugby-tackled it to the ground. When she worked with the dream, she identified with the rabbit, who said:

"Oh, no, not you again. Can't you see that I'm perfectly all right and can look after myself?"

Kathy then said that people often thought she couldn't cope, when in fact she was fine. When asked how people got that idea, she admitted that she liked to be fussed over, especially by men, but after a while she would feel claustrophobic and have to escape.

"I'm going through a massively changing time. I've propelled myself out of my comfortable (but caged) life because it was time to grow up, but it's difficult because I'll have to start knowing what I want and then say it to people."

AS GOOD AS GOLD

Sadie, who was orphaned and brought up by her sister only a few years older than her, had a recurring dream.

"I'm out walking with someone. It's dark and I see something bright and glittering in the dirt. It's money, gold coins. No one else sees them and I don't want to draw attention to them. I'm afraid someone will take them, so I cover them over."

Sadie's childhood had been bleak. She had suffered under the punitive regime of her sister, who was trapped into adult responsibility too early and lacked the natural love and compassion that an adult might have for a child in their charge. They had been very poor and Sadie had felt herself to be a burden to her sister.

Even though the dream demonstrated how unsafe Sadie felt, it was also a classic wish-fulfilment dream in that it gave her a glimpse of longed-for riches and well-being.

Imagine that you are these gold coins.
"I'm not just pennies. I'm money that's worth something."

What is gold?

"I'm valuable and I hold my worth. I'm a soft metal and very bright and shining. I can't be missed. [As herself] *Ah, I think this is the crux of it. I often don't value myself. There's a lack of self-worth at the core of me."*

Gold coins, why are you in the dirt?
"I've been neglected and thrown away. [As herself] *Oh, that's me and my sister! No matter what I did, it was always wrong, when really I was as good as gold."*

How come no one else sees you?
"Well, she hides me for fear her companion will be jealous. [As herself] *Oh, my sister was always jealous and hard on me. She always took away the good things."*

Here Sadie demonstrates how familiarity with the dream-catching process prompts spontaneous understanding of what a dream is about. She was able to see what her dream was based on and realize that she no longer needed to tolerate such put-downs. She also knew that she had dreamt this dream now because she was the "new girl" at her workplace and this had caused her familiar childhood insecurities to rise up again.

Nightmares

Often we are so thankful to wake from a nightmare that we immediately erase it from our memory. At other times, the horror of the images remains etched on the memory for ages. Nightmares signal that you are subconsciously working on a disturbing issue in your life. If you are able to remember the details of the nightmare, relief is at hand, for nightmares are never as bad as they appear. They are just dreams coming in hard and heavy in order wake you up. If you persistently ignore your needs, your dreams may start shouting at you. Bizarre and fearful scenarios may graphically illustrate parts of your personality that you constantly fail to acknowledge.

Cinema, literature, the Bible, art and many myths and legends allow us to see the unacceptable side of human nature in confrontations between heroes and villains. If we are to live our lives fully and responsibly, we need to own that we are both hero and villain, that the classic struggle between good and evil is being acted out within us. Prospero, the magician in Shakespeare's *The Tempest*, recognizes the dark side of his own nature when he says of the villainous Calaban: "This thing of darkness I acknowledge mine."

Natural instincts and impulses, although banished from our consciousness, will make themselves felt in our dreams. There we may suffer as victims or witness ourselves as murderers and torturers. Forbidden behaviours are often perpetrated in dreams by a character other than ourselves. We may wake up feeling persecuted and victimized.

Sally, a woman in her fifties, dreamt of torture scenes.

"I am witnessing terrible cruelties. In one scene, men like SS officers are operating on a young woman's stomach and she is saying, in extreme self-abasement, 'I'll breathe as little as possible' – as if to draw breath is a privilege to which she is not entitled."

After she had identified with the young woman and her pain, Sally said:

"I've remembered now what was hurting me over Christmas. I felt almost continuous pain in my stomach, but it all stopped when the stress of looking after everybody and all the arrangements had ended."

Let's stay with the dream for the moment. What are these men to you?

"They are terribly frightening – exactly like what's shown in films."

(Here Sally realized that she felt like the dream victim: she didn't protest when put upon, but got a pain in her gut instead. She acknowledged that she was torturing herself and needed to speak out more.)

At times emotional pain becomes so great that we dare not speak of it or allow it to be seen. It becomes a shameful thing, leaking into our every movement. The contractions needed to hold on or hold back can become chronic and might even restrict our vital organs, making us prone to heart disease or nervous disorder. This destructive process can be so slow that we don't realize what is happening until we become ill or reach the end of our tether. Dreams will reflect most of this, since they deal with our immediate concerns, processing the toxic waste of our emotions. They are a template upon which we project the inexpressible. They provide a virtual reality where we can work through our storms of pent-up feeling. After any trauma or difficult event, our dreams will start processing our dissatisfaction and unfinished business.

Children's dreams

Often larger than life, stark drama frequently inhabits children's dreams and nightmares. When taught how to make sense of their dreaming, children quickly come to see dreams as a support, an essential part of themselves that allows them to say what they need to be said. With parental support they learn how to face their monsters, sending them back from whence they came. A "nasty" dream can give them an opportunity to express their aggression creatively and become empowered by facing their fear. Sensitive dream-catching will support a child to express his or her needs, discharge hurts and move on with a lighter heart.

ANDREW'S DREAM

Helen was asked to see a ten-year-old boy who was persistently stealing. His parents had separated several months earlier and he was finding it difficult to cope with the upheaval. He was living with his father and missing his mother dreadfully. He found coming to see Helen difficult and strange, and couldn't talk about what was troubling him. When asked if he had dreams, he said he had one that came quite a lot. Again, he couldn't talk about it, so Helen suggested he draw it. He drew a large hollow tree with sparse leaves.

Helen invited him to describe himself as the tree.
"I'm a tree with a big hole inside."

How does it feel for you, tree, to have a big hole inside?
"It hurts."

Is that how you feel – as if you have a big hole inside?
[Nods and becomes tearful]

Can you think of anything that might help that hurt?
"Sweeties!"

This is why he was stealing money – to buy sweets to try to take away the emptiness he was feeling. He then became more forthcoming, working with and around this image, looking at how the hole had got there (a branch had broken off) and what he needed from his parents to help him deal with all the hurt.

Of course, his parents were hurting too and were not very available for him at the time. Talking within the sessions eventually enabled him to express how he felt and eventually he managed to let his parents know more about what he needed. Over time, the stealing stopped.

RUTH'S DREAM

A nine-year-old girl, troubled by a new relationship her mother had begun, asked to see a counsellor as she felt she couldn't talk to her mother any more. In waking fantasy, through sand play, she made up the following story.

"There is this lagoon and in it is a whale and a swan lives on it too. There is a crocodile living on the bank. The swan and the whale love each other, but the swan is not very happy because the whale and the crocodile are friends. The swan doesn't like the crocodile and feels very sad because she can't swim under water the way the whale and crocodile can."

Ruth wept as she absorbed the fact that her mother and her new friend had a life she didn't have access to. After this session she was able to tell her story to her mother, who then understood how difficult it was for her daughter to see her share her affections with someone else when she had had her mum to herself for so many years.

This type of story-telling is a form of conscious dreaming and demonstrates how powerfully children can use symbols to express their concerns. Parents need to recognize, however, that children's dreams are private affairs. If your child shares a dream with you, treat it carefully. Don't blunder in with jolly reassurances. Explore the dream at the child's own pace, following their interest. Encourage them to work out their story in their own way. Support whatever feelings arise with recognition and respect. Don't tell them that this is not the way it is. It is for them, and they will find their way through it if you patiently pace along with them.

Dreams of loss and death

One of life's heaviest burdens involves having to adjust to loss and death and deal with the empty space they leave inside. Most of us distract ourselves from this void by keeping busy or seeking out entertainment. Few of us have positive training in how to be alone or satisfied with our own company. This, perhaps, is why we feel so bereft when change and its accompanying feelings of loss can no longer be kept at bay. Dreams of loss and death can be seen as opportunities for dreamers to explore their fears about mortality.

ALAN'S DREAM

A man telephoned the radio dreamline saying that he had woken up crying. In his dream he was telling his mother that he was going to die. (In reality, he was dying of AIDS and had not yet found a way to tell her.) He said he felt alone and unable to say his goodbyes. Telling the dream enabled him, for the first time, to share his dilemma with someone else, which at least gave him a little relief. He was also able to see that perhaps he was depriving both his mother and himself of precious time together.

Although he'd gained some emotional release from weeping in his dream, he was still holding on to his sadness and distress. If this man were to work his dream further, perhaps talking to his mother in waking fantasy, he may have found the courage to choose a different path. As it was, he felt grateful for the opportunity to talk, if only briefly, and we hope he acted on the advice to seek out further help for himself.

This person's experience shows that when we are stuck, uncomfortable or unhappy, not daring to express our emotions fully, they will become active in our dreams, affording some emotional relief. Better to feel pain, hurt, anger or sadness in dreams than risk humiliation or rejection in real life. However, by acting on the messages given in dreams, we can learn to rescue ourselves.

During times of bereavement we may wake up sobbing with no memory of a dream. Our dreams are doing their work of enabling us to grieve while simultaneously allowing us to sleep and block out some of our pain. Dreams that do surface should be explored matter of factly, without getting caught up in fear and trembling. This is best done with someone who can encourage a dreamer to stay in the present and support them to look at whatever the dream is presenting to them.

TERENCE'S DREAM

Some dreams about death may appear to have no connection with the dreamer's reality. They seem to come out of the blue, as happened with Terence. He called Helen's phone-in after having a dream that disturbed him greatly. In the dream he had killed his mother. He could not understand what had made him dream such a thing because in real life he had been devoted to her and spent many years looking after her. As we worked, it transpired that he was very much like his mother: he helped other people and gave up his time for them, just as she had done for him. He found very little time for himself because he put himself out so much for others.

It is only natural to feel resentful about looking after others at such a large cost to ourselves. In fact, this mothering part of Terence was costing him dear and needed to be reined in. He could do with some mothering himself.

While the meaning of this dream was fairly obvious, that may not always be the case. When we feel trapped, dreams may invite us to liberate ourselves by presenting bizarre or disturbing images. These exaggerations of what we need to notice shock us into paying attention. In Terence's case, his unconscious frustration with his position made him dream about killing his mother, which left him shocked, worried and needing to understand what it was all about. It was only when he looked more closely at how this symbolic mothering behaviour actually belonged to him and was costing too much of his time and energy that he realized he needed to moderate it – not kill it off totally, but certainly curb it enough to prevent it from being a deadening influence in his own life.

CHANGE FOR THE BETTER
Tibetan Buddhists believe that the process of dying needs special attention – that all the little "deaths" of life are training for the final letting go. They believe how we die, how conscious we are during that last journey, will affect whether and how we reincarnate again. Whatever you believe, it seems to follow that if we make good endings in life, we are freer to progress whole-heartedly to the next beginning. When our endings are messy, we enter new experiences guarded and weighed down with the clutter of what has been left unsaid, the baggage of unexpressed feeling and the heaviness of regret.

Most mystical and religious systems believe that death is the final earthly phase of moving on to another existence. They point to the naturalness of death, likening it to winter in the progression of the seasons. Witnessing nature's eternal cycle may give us the courage and energy to move vigorously on into old age.

None of us knows for sure where life will take us, especially as plans may not come to fruition in the way we hoped they would. Some things turn out better than expected, some worse. Eventually we come to realize that the only certainty we can rely on is change. With each "sling and arrow of outrageous fortune" we are forced to view our lives from a different perspective, learn something new and develop our resources. Our dreams can help us do this. When we recognize them as reflections of our inner concerns, they can begin to help us make sense of what we are dealing with and enable us to be true to ourselves along the way.

Working with dreams of death and dying

1 Work with a nightmare in the same way that you would work with a dream.

2 Tell it in the present, as it's happening, and describe the associations and feelings it evokes.

3 Go to the part of the dream that has the most impact for you. (If you feel afraid, remind yourself that it is just a dream, a message that needs unravelling.)

4 Be the various parts of the dream:
- Identify with the person, animal or thing who is suffering or dying and tell the dream through their eyes.
- What do they need to say to those left behind?
- What is causing their death?
- What do they need from you or others?

5 Ask yourself :
- What is changing in my life at present?
- What is dying in my life?
- What do I need to let go of?

6 You may not yet feel you are ready, but your dream may be preparing you to let go of something. Talk it over with a trusted friend. You don't have to stay alone with this.

Dreams and post-traumatic stress

Throughout this book we have demonstrated how repressed emotions about difficult and painful situations often surface in dreams. If dreamers have persistent nightmares linked to the real-life traumas they have survived, they may be reluctant to work with their dreams for fear of reliving the horrifying experiences once again. This is a real dilemma because unless they work through the experience it will continue to visit them in their dreams. Those suffering horrific dreams in the aftermath of trauma can benefit from the on-going support of a professional worker. Within a therapeutic relationship they will eventually be able to recognize that their dreams are re-creating horrors for a purpose (usually to get them to let go of their fears, face up to their losses and see that now they are not so alone).

Working through dreams involving post-traumatic stress requires a skill and delicacy that only experienced dream-workers can offer. The following transcript and synopses of two subsequent dreams are included to illustrate the healing power of dreams. They should not be used as templates for novice work in this field.

MEMORIES OF WAR

As an example, an old soldier suffering disturbing dreams about his wartime experiences might find them too painful to investigate in the usual way, so a dialogue could be set up between the dreamer and the dream.

[Soldier to his nightmares] *"Why do you keep plaguing me and upsetting me?"*
[Dream] *"Because you remember me and call me to you."*
"I don't want you. Go away!"

[Therapist] **What exactly is it that you don't want?**
[Soldier] *"All the pain and hurt. All that violence and anger.* [To the dream] *What do I have to do to get you to leave me alone?"*
[Dream] *"Honour me."*
"I don't know what you mean."
[Dream] *"Bury me with honour."*
"How can I do that? It was a useless war. So much loss of life. [To the therapist] *I feel so angry I don't know where to put myself."*
[Therapist] **Who are you angry with?**
"Them! All of them! All the bastards who put us out there. The Hooray Henrys and pen-pushing Peters. The lot of them."

Tell them what you think of them.
(The soldier speaks furiously and at length until spent. Then he stops, looking a bit embarrassed.)

You certainly got up a head of steam there.
"I didn't know all that was in me. It's not like me to be angry. I enjoyed giving them a piece of my mind, though... I feel quieter now. That's what I need – some quietness, some peace of mind."

Let's go back to your dream: what does it have to say about all this?
[As dream] *"I didn't ask you to honour the people who made the war but to honour yourself and your compatriots. That's why I kept presenting them to you."*
[Soldier, weeping quietly] *"I have always felt so ashamed, so frightened, not brave and glorious... The memories... the dreams... are so awful."*

Is there anything more you could do now to honour yourself and them?
"Bury them... I need to say goodbye properly, without pretending. Yes, I can imagine them buried, I could give them a nice grave, let them, and me, rest in peace."

Rewriting dreams

Another way of dealing with repetitive frightening dreams that feel too dangerous to explore is to rewrite them as if you are a scriptwriter (which, of course, you are). Go back into your dream and imagine a better ending for yourself. Allow your fantasy to unravel a script that gives you a way out, or some support to deal with your difficulty in the dream. Talking this process over with a dream-catcher or therapist can help you to trust your rewrite.

We stay victims to aggressive situations in dreams until we honour whatever is provoking them. It's only when we start to own our feelings and give them their rightful expression that we can face our night horrors safe in the full knowledge that whatever has happened to us before can never happen to us in that way again. We are older, wiser and now and – we hope – more able to mobilize support in our lives.

Dreams in the aftermath of abuse

Victims of violence and abuse often suffer great shame about their ordeal, which makes it difficult for them to talk about or access their deepest feelings. When a client feels safe enough within a therapeutic relationship, the dreaming process can support them through their post-traumatic stress rather than just become a perpetuation of it. Many people have been assisted through a process similar to those outlined in the box above. After working through their dreams in this way, they can start changing. They will feel less helpless – more in charge of themselves. Eventually, they will bring current dreams to sessions and work on them directly.

MANDY

A young woman living with her partner and beloved horse, Mandy has for many years presented an image of calm, capable control to the outside world. Few would guess that she is a survivor of horrific sexual and emotional abuse. From the age of three, when she was abandoned on a doorstep with her baby brother, Mandy has learned to keep her feelings under control. All through the endless rejections of the adoption system, she watched impassively as possible mummies and daddies reached out for her baby brother, only to let him go when they realized that Mandy was part of the package.

The children were eventually adopted, but it was then that the cruelty and horror began for Mandy. While her little brother enjoyed the affections of both his adoptive parents, she was sacrificed to the sexual obsessions of her new father. At seventeen Mandy left home and made her own way in the world. Miraculously, she retained her sweetness and a deep concern for the welfare of others. Externally she shows herself responsible and unflappable, choosing a career path that has taken her into a position of considerable authority. Internally, however, she constantly struggles with the demons of her childhood, which can be aroused by an unthinking touch or moment of intimacy. She manages to cope only by distancing herself from people and lavishing affection on her horse, the only thing she really trusts to be a loyal and safe companion.

Mandy knew that she needed help and time to heal. She wanted a place where she could withdraw into herself when the going got tough. She was recommended to a gestalt training programme open to long-term clients who wished to pursue their therapy intensively within a training group. At first, some people's "work" triggered her emotions too strongly – she feared losing control and would flee the room. However she found most of the group experience reassuring and supportive. After a couple of years, she felt more secure and could better resist her urge to flee.

Mandy's dreams stand out like beacons on her path. They have enabled her to face her demons and show her distress within the group. The enormity of what she has endured gradually dawned on us as we witnessed her struggle to confront her nightmares. We feel privileged to support her in her slow and painful recovery. Through dream-catching, Mandy has been able to talk to her abuser and express her pain and anger. Her drive for a less tortured life has propelled her into facing her feelings about her own body, and her dreams have provided a path for healing. Through them she has gradually come to feel more kindly towards herself and more accepting of her need to give and receive affection and love. As Mandy's healing continued, she became able to talk more freely about herself. One morning she telephoned Helen, saying that she had watched a film she knew she shouldn't. She had known it would give her a hard time afterwards, so she kept awake as long as she could. When she eventually fell asleep she had a dream about good and bad. (Significant phrases appear in bold type to amplify essential links.)

MANDY'S FIRST DREAM

"I'm sitting outside with you [Helen] *and Deita* [a previous trainee who had also suffered much cruelty in her life]. *Deita covers her face all over and is talking in a language I don't know. You are saying to her, 'This isn't you, Deita. Something's taken over your body.' You try to talk to her but can't get through. Deita comes over and passes whatever it is to me and you say, 'It's OK, Mandy, you're strong enough to take this.' A force then lifts me over to you and wants me to lie on top of you. I can't control this and it drops me down on your lap. You cuddle me and I feel OK. I feel really nice and know that I've wanted this sort of thing for a long time. Then everything changes as the force rises up again and suddenly you are on my lap. I am hugging and supporting you but it doesn't feel right. Your left breast is exposed and I am not comfortable.*

"Suddenly there is a coach careering down on us at 100 mph. I can see clearly that it's going to kill us both. You shoot off to the right and I go to the left. I'm running as fast as possible and the coach follows me. I am crying because I'm sure you're dead. The coach goes until it runs out of steam, then I go back and find you wrapped in a plastic bag. You say, 'I've fallen in hot oil but I'm OK.' Next I'm in a car on the motorway and I step out of the car and start running a marathon."

Be Deita.

"I am possessed by an unknown entity in my body and I have no control over how I am presenting myself to you. All I know is that I have to cover myself up and talk a language I don't know."

What do you make of that, Mandy?

"Well, it obviously relates to the abuse and it's possible that it's how I live my life now. I don't have any feeling about it."

Be Helen in the dream.

"I'm sitting on the chair and I do not recognize Deita in the form she's in, how she's presenting herself. I'm not going to be able to get through to her but I know Mandy could. Deita's message is totally directed at Mandy. **I am powerless really and can just support Mandy to deal**

with what's going to happen. I'm frightened. I'm used to having control and I don't know what is going to happen."
(This is a pretty good description of how the therapeutic process is sometimes experienced by the client.)

[Mandy as herself] *"I am like that in the way things present in my life. I don't have control or know why things are happening to me. I have no control over how I am affected or what the outcome will be."*
(Reader, can you hear the echoes of the past? This is a re-creation, an accurate description of just how it was for Mandy as a young girl. Listen for these echoes throughout this dream.)

"In the dream I see that Helen's not going to be able to get through to Deita and I realize I've no choice but to help Deita myself. It's my natural response to rescue her, to try to get her away, to distract her and find the real her. This is OK initially, then she grabs my arms and puts what's in her in me. She's getting rid of all this crap and putting it into me."
(This has been Mandy's whole therapeutic task – to rescue herself from her memories and bad feelings. This is a near-perfect description of what happens in the cycle of abuse. In attempting to free herself from the horror done to them, an innocent victim will act it out and dump it on an innocent other.)

"In the dream what I didn't say was, 'It's not OK to have done that without asking my permission'."
(Once again, this is a re-creation. It's just what she was unable to say to her adoptive father.)

"Last night I couldn't go to sleep. Just like those childhood days, I kept thinking that there were people in the room. I kept saying to myself, 'I've got to keep my eyes open.' I had to do this as a child. Night after night, I'd wait for daylight. Last night I couldn't go downstairs for a drink or anything. I was too afraid to go down. I said to Pru [her partner], 'Only Helen can keep me safe.' I had to keep thinking of you, trying to keep hold of the vision of that time when you hugged me in the group."
(A reference to a rare occasion when she had briefly allowed herself to move closer Helen.)

"I felt that whatever was possessing me was inside me. I'm not sure whether it was evil or good, a real conflict of the two. Goodness had to fight evil and protect me. That was the spirit part. The other part was sexual – falling on top of you [Helen] was what 'it' wanted to do: it lifted me right off the floor. But goodness won over the bad and I fell with my head in your lap. It was really good. You held my head and I felt safe. You stroked my hair and gave me a hug and I felt like this is what I've wanted for all these years. Good delivered me to good. Then bad came and the whole thing swapped over and it became scary with you and your bare breast."

Be Helen in the dream.
"I'm just saying this is OK. It doesn't have to be bad or sexual."
[As Mandy] *"And knowing this, I can really rest."*
(It is important that Mandy give herself reassurance through being Helen in the dream.)

Be the energy that flips things over.
"I am really powerful. I have total control. I'm extreme force, the ultimate force you can meet. I can destroy and devastate everything I meet. You have to give in to me no matter who you are. I just want intense, short-lived power."
(This is exactly what she suffered and endured as a child.)

[Mandy as herself] **"It really has presented itself now. I can't avoid this. I've had such a fear of this rising up."**
(The feelings that this "it" represents are those that Mandy has been guarding herself and others from for most of her life.)

It's not only you that makes this sort of connection, Mandy. It's not only you who has these feelings. This is a graphic demonstration of what you suffered and this sort of energy comes up in intense intimacy anyway. Couples often have to deal with this sort of primal force and they don't know where it comes from. Often sado-masochistic feelings seem to arise from nowhere, but they are connected to the helplessness and excitement of childhood, when we were pushed around and treated as if we had no power at all.

Now be Helen when she was flipped over.

"I'm sitting on Mandy's lap. It's happened really quickly, so I'm not sure about what's going on. I know that I feel quite firm about who and what I am, and I need to be that because Mandy is not at all sure. She's out of control, so I need to be doubly in control to protect her even though I'm OK with what she's doing because I've got boundaries."

[Mandy to Helen] *"I did feel that you were very safe."*
(Here she is describing the good parent that she needed, as well as part of herself that has a positive identity and can look after herself.)

Helen in the dream, as you know, is part of you. Let's look at this part of you that despite the flipping over can keep firm, staying just where you are. Perhaps you don't have to control yourself so strictly? Perhaps now you can just take care of yourself? How would it be to own that for yourself?

"This can't sink in yet. I am so controlled that it seems so out of the question."

Well, you have never had a model like this in your life before. You did not get good parenting. You know that what we create in dreams indicates what is possible. This possibility may now start filtering through to your everyday life.

"Even though this is just a dream, it does make complete sense. Although as Helen in the dream my breast is exposed, it doesn't bother me – it's not sexual. Maybe I am offering that as a mother. I know it's just happened without thought. I'm just still, sitting there freely, waiting to see what Mandy does. I can't move anyway because Mandy's grip on me is so tight.
[As Mandy] *"I think this bare breast means it's sexual. What am I meant to do? This breast rubs against my cheek and I want to grab hold of it but I can't because it's a sexual thing. I am naturally close to you and then all the fear comes rushing in."*
(Here we see clearly a dilemma that is common in relationships generally. Many people long for the comfort represented by the breast, a comfort and safety that they pull back from for fear of it becoming sexual.)

And because you didn't know it was all right to cuddle up, you can't give yourself the comfort. You then have to face this coach roaring in at 100 mph. *"Yes. It's saying, 'My aim is to kill them, to totally set them apart.'"* (Mandy feels she must totally separate comfort and sexual behaviour so that one will not be contaminated by the other.)

Coach, who is driving you?
"It might be a man – I don't know. I get the feeling that it's Mandy as a man. I am being driven in absolute rage. All I can focus on is the two of them sitting there. I'm trying to hit them, especially Mandy, and I'll hit Helen in the process."

Why?
*"I don't like the two of them. I just hate them. (Passionately) **I absolutely hate you and I will kill you. My intention is to kill both of you.** [Pause] **That's it then… they've gone.**"*

You've wiped them out?
"I don't like the closeness they've got. I don't think it's right."

Is this the fine line between sex and comfort? Does closeness become so threatening that you have to drive a bus through it?
[Mandy as herself] *"I wonder if I'm unconsciously trying to destroy the relationship between you and me? Yes, of course…"*
[As the coach] *"I've got to get the hell out of here. I've just got to go."*
[As herself again] *"Then the bus hits."*

Tell me what happens to Helen?
"I leg it out from this bus. If I don't, I'm going to be killed. I have to leave Mandy and run for cover. I protect myself in a carrier bag and fall into this hot oil, although I'm not burnt."

Be the oil.
*"I am hot oil and I have to let Helen know that there is danger. I mustn't let her think that because she is in a carrier bag she is safe. **But Helen is not really backing off.**"*

152

[Mandy as herself] *"You see I've always lost everything I've got close to in my life."* (Weeps)

You shut down, because you are afraid of closeness, and then lose it?
"It's really difficult. I've never done this in my life... got this close to someone who knows so much about me."

But this time you haven't stayed alone. You're talking to me. Be Helen in the dream.
"I've run for cover and I'm protecting myself in a bag. The bus won't see me in a bag. It'll just think I'm a bag. I've gone very small, like the size of a baby, but really I'm an adult. My mentality is of my present age. Then Mandy finds me and I'm in this oil. It's hot oil. There's still danger as it's quite hot, but I'm not scalded by it."

Be the plastic bag.
"I'm not thick; I'm thinnish and ordinary. I can't be melted despite the oil... I've been left on the street by someone. I've been discarded. I can take the heat."
(This is a poignant description of Mandy. Despite being left on the street (discarded) by her mother, she can still take the heat.)

"Helen gets inside me and that's all right. I will protect her."
(Remember that Helen is the small, indestructible part of Mandy that has survived after being abandoned, the part she must protect no matter what.)

[Mandy as herself] *"I'll protect you whatever happens."*
(Mandy feels she has to say this to the real Helen because she fears that the dream is indicating that she is a danger to her and their relationship. She has taken the goodness of her relationship with Helen into her and needs to preserve it.)

"I know this dream is all about me giving you lots of power because I'm telling you everything. I know I'm OK with you. It's me I'm beginning to distrust because it's so new and has only just happened. All my life story's coming out in this one dream. My whole life has been about

*power. As soon as I'm afraid of being hurt, there's another part of
me that says it isn't going to let it happen."*

That makes sense. When you are treated so very badly, you learn at a deep
level to look after yourself, keeping guard and keeping people at a distance.
This dream is another milestone. In your dream you feel longings for closeness
along with your fears. You make the step towards closeness but you still can't
allow it. You allow yourself to get close to me, then you imagine that you will
hurt me or I will hurt you – both of us will be destroyed.

*"I always swore that I would never get close to you. When the other
trainees left the group, I saw how hurt they were, and I thought, 'No
one is going to hurt me in this way.' Now I look back and I realize that
they were simply saying goodbye in a healthy way, with all their feelings."*

So in the dream, although Helen is strong, she is also vulnerable? Be her.

*"Mandy, who is very upset now because she fears I am dead, finds me
and opens the bag. She says, 'Are you OK?' and I say, 'I'm fine and this
isn't your fault.' I check my body and am amazed that I'm not hurt.
I look up at Mandy."*

What is the quality of that look?

*"Amazement. I can't believe all this. 'Just get me out of this bag.' Mandy
lifts me out of the bag and I grow back to my normal size."*
(In reality, only Mandy is able to lift herself out of this abandoned place.)

So when that huge coach ploughed through, you became incredibly small and
put yourself back into that abandoned place, the bag that was left?

"Yes, and I say, 'To lift me out will allow you to take your proper age.'"

So, Mandy, your natural healthy self has been put into the abandoned bag
where you can hide yourself for safety. Lifting yourself out can give you your
full life?

*"I think I should be feeling different. I feel numb and unemotional.
It's all very interesting intellectually, like reading a book. I know I can
consolidate and do things differently, but the step of reading and then
putting it into practice…"*

(This response is not surprising, as Helen has been working too hard to get Mandy to make the connections she can see. She is talking too much and hurrying the process.)

"I am relieved that Helen in the dream is OK. I was distraught and devastated that somebody I had got so close to had gone out of my life and that I was responsible."
(Once again, here is confirmation that Helen in the dream represents the part of Mandy that was abandoned yet has survived intact despite the abuse. This statement echoes the feelings of the little girl who thought she was the cause of her own abandonment. (Children often believe it is their fault when something goes wrong in the family.) Mandy in real life has been zealously protecting others as well as herself from the hurt that can come from intimacy.)

"I pick Helen up. I'm really pleased and feel so deep and raw because I was led to believe that she was dead. Then I get a vehicle and drive miles away from her on a busy road. I leave the car and walk up on to a wooden plateau. I can see miles and miles of road ahead of me and there's water. I start running."

What's your message to the Helen you've left behind?
"It's not fair to you: you've done your part. It's time for me to give you back your life. I'm running this marathon because the close-ness and impact is too unbearable."

So you get back on the road to the old familiar ending? Could there be an alternative ending?
"I could stop running and turn back to the [Helen] part of me that is still alive, secure and safe... That's unbearable as well."

What's unbearable?
"To stay in the warmth, cosiness and relief. I really don't know. It's all unbearable because... because..."
(Here Mandy again shows the difficulty experienced by people who have been hurt in coming into close relationships again. It seems obvious that she should take whatever comfort is available, but her dilemma is that if she does "come

in from the cold", she will reactivate all the old feelings of longing that she has had to hide away. On top of that, the comfort and warmth of being cared for will also bring home to her how long she has been out in the cold. All the years of distance and aloneness. Better to stay with what she knows. But that's not possible now as she has moved on too far and is facing the fact that her numb isolation is no longer as comfortable for her as it was. She is wanting more from her life.)

What does Helen say?
"Stop it! Stop running! I'm sad Mandy is doing this. We've been through so much, survived this far, and I don't want her to go. I think she'll come back. Even though so much has happened, I still feel strong and safe for her."
(The healthy, loving, vulnerable part of her that she has projected on to Helen has not died: it is still strong and still has hope.)

"I think because of her strength, the good will will take over and she will come back to what she knows. I can't call her back. I know she has to do this. I know that she'll come back because she can't leave something that's vulnerable for long."
(This is a total replay in symbolic form of what Mandy has already survived. Her mother did leave something that was vulnerable, and now Mandy has to rescue that abandoned part of herself.)

Be Mandy.
"I can see this road, all these cars. I get over the road. I feel that I could run for ever. I could run like this for the rest of my life. The running feels so comfortable, so natural, and when I'm running in this place and I'm alone, I can slip right off and I don't have to think of anything other than the trees and what I'm seeing. It's a total distraction."

From what?
"From closeness. My running is as powerful as the wanting to stay. It's easier and less painful than staying. I think the running is a physical thing and the staying is all my emotions. That's it."

[Noticing that the real Helen is upset by this image] *"**Helen** [in the dream] is sitting with all the emotions."*

Be Helen in the dream.
"I feel battered and exhausted, but the oil is keeping me warm. I need to grow, to move on from here, but I need Mandy to come back and do this. It's an equal dilemma: the energy and power are equal. I'm as strong as the runner but I'm hoping my warmth will overpower the physical. I have to sit here... What if she doesn't come back? I will be left here as long as she's running this marathon. I'm just a little more insulated than she is."

And what would be the end of this movie?
"I will find a way of growing and I will get ahead of Mandy and meet her. I will confront her so she cannot run any more. She won't be able to pass me. She can't run away from me any more. I'm here whether she likes it or not. She can't get away from me. I'll face her and that will melt her."
(Here are echoes of the abandoned child needing to find and confront her abandoning mother who did a "runner", but this time it is different. Mandy now affirms a sense of herself when she says, "I'm here whether she likes it or not." She knows that her integrity and determination will get her through so that she can at last melt.)

[Mandy as herself] *"Helen's out of the bag but still insulated by the oil on her body (**a bit like a baby**). Her mental age is like mine now; the physical isn't relevant."*

[As Helen in the dream] *"I'll grow the body with will-power. I can survive in the world."*
(This, of course, is what Mandy did: she survived by will-power and is now at a point where she can "grow" her body for herself – with love. Then there comes a recognition of the connection and conflict between the two parts of her.)

[As Helen in the dream] *"But my feelings are powerful and passion-ate and the running part doesn't recognize this."*

(The real Helen uses reality to challenge the dream runner.)
Mandy, you can't run for ever. You're going to get old.
"I want both parts to help each other out, to meet."
(Here Mandy clearly expresses the agony of those who have been abused and had to dissociate their bodies from their feelings in order to survive in the world. They walk around in solitary confinement until they feel safe enough to release and "regrow" themselves.)

[To the real Helen] *"I'm doing this as quick as I can by sticking to my therapy and trusting you."*

Trust your natural process. Stay open to this knowledge that you can protect yourself by running when you need to. You've already done most of the work. Let yourself relax a bit.

This proved to be impossible. Over the next thirty-six hours, Mandy was in a turmoil of intense physical and emotional pain as the ghosts of her past tormented her. She felt rage, self-doubt and shame. She was unable to relate, speak or be touched. She could feel the full force of her need for love, yet at the same time contracted and recoiled from it. It was no longer an unconscious action. Now she knew what she was struggling with, the old familiar feelings surfaced and she felt powerless to deal with them. She experienced intense longing and great fear as she imagined the damage her feelings could do to others, especially to her therapist, Helen. She recognized that a lot of the things she was thinking and fearing about Helen actually belonged to her adoptive mother, who, although not personally guilty of abusing her, had sacrificed her to "him". She also remembered how her adoptive mother's language had been peppered with sexual innuendo.

More pieces of Mandy's personal jigsaw were now beginning to fall into place. She struggled with her intense longings to be held and cared for by Helen – her therapist – and remembered feeling suffocated and repulsed on the only occasion she could recall being held by her adoptive mother. She was assailed by her old defences to intimacy and sexuality. She wrote to Helen, explaining how difficult all these things were and how she felt awkward and exposed at having shown so much of the darkness inside her. In telephone sessions over the next few days, Mandy was able to voice some of her pain, and Helen was able to reassure her that she was neither going to abandon nor reject her because of what she was struggling with. Perhaps most importantly, Helen reassured Mandy that she was not going to act on or take advantage of these confidences, that she was now perfectly safe, and that it was natural for her to be feeling all these things. Indeed, it was essential for her to feel this way in order to heal and get through to a better place where her defensive self could stay with her emotional self and keep it safe, rather than cutting it off and running away from it.

This last part of the work can be seen as a reflection of Mandy's early life experience. She was abandoned as a little girl, but now in her dream it is she who is running away from her feelingful child: to stay with her hurts too much. Remember what Mandy said in the dream to Helen and the child she represented: "It's not fair to you: you've done your part. It's time for me to give you back your life." Yet again, this echoes the agony of an abandoning mother who is struggling to do the best for her child – hoping to give her a better life without the stress and strain of hurtful emotions.

Mandy's dream offered her a testing opportunity to do it differently this time around. There is still some way to go, but one of her greatest battles has already been won. It will just take some time to sort out the peace.

Over the few weeks that followed, Mandy continued to have dreams but blocked many of them out. She then chose to attend a five-day residential training group, confident that she would feel safe enough to work through whatever arose. There she caught two dreams, which followed directly on from the first.

MANDY'S SECOND DREAM
"I'm in a coach. It's the coach of the first dream and it's being driven crazily and dangerously. My dog is with me and is being thrown around: there's nothing I can do to help him. Suddenly he is thrown out of the coach, but the coach careers on. I manage to get out myself and rush to where the dog is lying at the edge of the road. I know that he is really badly hurt and I must get him to a vet. His leg is split open to the bone and just hanging there. I gather him up and run for ages until I get to the vet's. It's full of other people and animals and I just can't stay there, so I have to leave him. I wake up from the dream feeling dreadful."

As Mandy worked through this dream in the group, she came to realize that it represented progress for her because she had achieved several things in it. She had managed to get treatment for the innocent part of her that had been dreadfully hurt, despite all the other people at the vet's (who represented all the other participants on the residential course). She had rescued and cuddled her dog (her injured self) in a way she could only think about in her previous dream. She was able to take this hurt part of herself to a crowded surgery and, through further working, found that her dog didn't die. Although lame, he would be able to go home with her and live a good life. Not least, she had got off the coach and was no longer running away.

MANDY'S THIRD DREAM

"I am helping a client and concentrating on listening when a woman walks in and keeps interrupting us. I feel really angry and protective of my client. I want to concentrate on her, but suddenly my rage really takes over and I scream at the interloper to get out."

Working with this dream, Mandy felt disappointed that her anger at the interloper, whom she recognized as a human version of the coach in her previous dreams, had pushed the client – her own needy part – back into a withdrawn, unreachable place.

Mandy took the part of the client in the dream and felt how powerfully the protective anger she had expressed shoved her back into a blocked-off and injured place. In the client role she was able to express her distress only by sitting silently, cut off, with bowed head. In this all-too-familiar posture, she remembered what it had been like as a child, coping all alone with her bruises, and she told us a little of how she had had to look after herself. Helen placed a hand on her shoulder, and as Mandy didn't flinch, Helen then circled her shoulders lightly with her arms. Mandy stiffened momentarily, then softened and allowed herself to be held for a few seconds. She then pulled away, but a few seconds later asked to be held again. This time she allowed herself to lean a little on Helen, her tears streaming as she surrendered to the grief of her lost childhood.

Through these dreams Mandy had progressed from projecting her injured self on to Helen and abandoning her, to placing her vulnerability on to her dog and rescuing him, to letting us know about her own hurt and isolation and allowing someone to get close enough to comfort her. The part of her that kept her away from closeness had moved from being an out-of-control coach to an interloper who could be dealt with. She had come in from the cold at last. Over the next two days Mandy's face opened, showing her joy as well as her vulnerability, and she allowed her fun side to emerge without cloaking it in her usual cynicism. Her dreams had given her a way through.

Working through difficult dreams with a companion is like having a hand to hold in the dark. Unfortunately, some people are dismissive of counselling and therapy, claiming that they add to human misery rather than relieve it. Obviously, they or someone they love has never been badly traumatized. Anyone who has witnessed the night terrors of a trauma victim could not hold this opinion. I remember one of my trainees telling me of long nights she spent with a pillow over her head trying to shut out the screams and shouts of her father as he regularly struggled to survive in his dreams – the after-effects of the First World War.

The days when traumatized people were locked in asylums or hid their terrors by gritting their teeth, swallowing sedatives or drowning themselves in drink are long gone. Thankfully, present times are more supportive of the need to work through the aftermath of trauma, uncomfortable as that may be for all of us. ✩

9

TROUBLE SHOOTING

D ream-catching is relatively straightforward and, with practice, becomes almost second nature. At the beginning, however, you might encounter some obstacles due to personal resistance and blind spots, or lack of familiarity with our methods. This chapter aims to help you to get the most out of the process, identifying common difficulties and offering suggestions and exercises to overcome them. If you remain unable to solve a difficulty, further support is available from Dream Catchers' telephone helpline (see page 186).

Familiarity with the method outlined so far will help you to become innovative and creative in your own dream-working. Dreams are merely templates, skeletons of linked associations and symbolic representations, whose meanings become more apparent through exploration and investigation. Let go of your preconceptions and take the courage to look at parts of yourself that you might previously have found difficult to acknowledge.

Knowing where to start

A dream is multi-faceted, each part in its own way reflecting an aspect of a particular theme in your life. The deeper meaning of the dream runs like a thread throughout the dream script, and wherever you choose to start, the theme will soon become apparent. What at first seem to be disconnected parts are offering you numerous paths to access your dream message.

There are several ways to unpack a dream. The most thorough is to identify with each part of it (see Chapter 4 for a detailed description of this process). You could start with the element of the dream that you are most curious about, the one that holds most energy for you, whether it be positive or negative. Identifying with this part of the dream first could lead you directly into the issues you are presently dealing with. Alternatively, you might start with a missing aspect of the dream, for example:

"I'm driving a car with only three wheels."

Ask yourself where the other wheel is and continue in daydream mode from that point.

"Well, I was attached until my driver hit the kerb, then I loosened and eventually rolled away. The driver was going at such speed he didn't notice me leaving. Oh!"

What is it?

"My husband is having a really hard time at present and can barely talk to me. He's so busy trying to sort out his business. I'm feeling more and more alone. I've even been thinking of leaving him. The other day I caught myself wondering how long it would take him to notice if I were gone. Life feels a bit precarious at the moment."

Learn to dig deep

Some dreams are more difficult to understand than others: they remain a mystery until their last symbol is examined and owned. With others, the key to understanding may be accessed only through hearing the spontaneous words the dreamer uses to describe an object, or by listening to the conversation held between different aspects of the dream story. In our experience, the meaning of all dreams eventually becomes apparent through the dream-catcher patiently weaving between dream imagery and real-life logic. The lemmings dream in Chapter 5 is a good example of this. That dreamer had made an assumption about a dream image (lemmings tumbling over a cliff). It was only when he took in the fact that they had wings that he saw they were not lemmings after all. He then realized that if he would but spread his own metaphorical wings, he too could fly. He was not a lemming either.

Dreamers can get caught up in the labyrinth of a dream story, losing their ability to see beyond its macabre or fantastical imagery. If they step out of the dream and apply their common sense to the real-life properties of a particular image, the challenge of the dream may suddenly become clear.

Working with uncomfortable images

One of the hurdles you may face is a reluctance to explore symbols that seem to represent an unpleasant or unacceptable aspect of yourself. If this happens, you may need to talk the dream over with someone you trust, or use a professional dream-catcher to help you look beyond the superficial meaning of the symbols. For example, a dreamer presenting a dream about a gun might be asked:

How are you like a gun?
"But I'm not like a gun. How could you suggest that?"

(Here the dream-catcher needs to persist even in the face of resistance and affront.)
Take a risk: be the gun.
"What do you mean 'be the gun'?"

Describe yourself as if you were a gun.
(If this is still too difficult for the dreamer, you might need to lighten the risk.)

Describe a gun to me.
"A gun is a violent thing. It kills people. I'm not like that."

Yes, that is one of a gun's functions. Let's look more closely at all its uses.
"Well, it could be used for defence or hunting, to kill animals for sport or food."

So as a gun you have positive uses as well as negative ones?
[Reluctantly] *"I suppose so...yes. I don't understand where all this is leading."*

Let's go to the properties of a gun. What are you made of?
"A hard, shiny metal."

And how are you made?
"I need a craftsman, someone who knows how to deal with metal and knows how to design me to make me safe."

To make you safe?
"Yes. A gun is a dangerous thing and needs to be handled carefully."

What is metal?
"I think it comes from the ground. It has to be mined, then refined, heated, moulded and polished so it can be used."

And it needs a craftsman to do all this?
"Yes, in order to make it safe so it won't blow up in your face."

So a gun can kill but can also be useful if handled carefully?

"Yes... I'm beginning to see what you mean."
Tell me more.
"Well, I suppose I'm a bit like this."

How?
"I come from a mining village – coal, not metal. It was pretty rough really, and I suppose you could say I've been refined by going through university. It doesn't take much to make me lose my temper. It's got me into trouble in the past, but I'd never kill anyone."

Let's look at the gun in the context of this dream. Where are you, gun, and what are you doing in the dream? Try to identify with the gun now as if you're acting a part and giving it a voice.
"I'm hidden in the dream. This person stumbles upon me and is quite shocked."

Shocked?
"Yes – you see, I'm not where you would expect me to be."

Where are you?
"I'm in a fridge – I suppose you're going to ask me what a fridge is now?

You guessed it.
"It's a place to keep food in. It keeps food for longer, so it doesn't go off."

Say that again.
"A fridge keeps food for longer so it doesn't go off."

I notice you pull a face there. Can you tell me what happens when you say this?
"It's sort of funny that the gun has to be treated carefully so that it does-n't go off, and now I'm talking about food being kept in a fridge so it doesn't go off."

What does this mean for you? Is there some part of you that you're cooling down so it doesn't go off?
"Yes, there is! I'm trying to stay cool so that I don't spoil things at work.

There's a new guy who presses my buttons so hard and it's getting to be a struggle for me… so much so that I don't want to go into work any more. I don't know what to do. The job suits me and I need it for my bread and butter, but I just don't know how to handle this guy."

So now we see how you are like this gun?
"Yes, you've got me there. But what am I going to do about it?"

At last the dreamer has gained some understanding of what his dream is about. However, awareness alone may not do anything much to relieve his real-life predicament. He may need to work on further, as demonstrated below.

Working on from a dream

Gaining understanding of a dream's meaning is a vital step towards utilizing its wisdom. With the gun example above, there are several possible ways forward. This dreamer could now focus on his real-life situation and imagine talking to the new guy at work, giving full expression to his discontent and criticism. Doing this in the session would probably release some of the pressure caused by his pent-up feelings. In the absence of a facilitator to witness and support an imaginary conversation, the dreamer could cool down by writing a letter to the new guy. Sending the letter would not be wise, but the symbolic burning or ripping up of the letter might help the dreamer to distance himself from the discord. When powerful feelings are unexpressed or not put into their correct context, they might be vented on others, usually those less strong than ourselves.

Openly expressing feelings within the safety of a dream-catching session will help to validate the dreamer, relieve some of the internal pressure and clear enough space to look at alternative ways of resolving conflict. After working through a possible conversation, the gun dreamer may come to recognize who the new person reminds him of. Some unfinished business is surfacing that really belongs in the past, perhaps relating to his relationship with a younger, brighter sibling? After putting himself in the other man's shoes, the dreamer may come to better understand what he is re-enacting. Speaking from the other person's perspective might help him to appreciate that person's position.

In dream-catching, just as in dreams themselves, anything is possible. Whatever emerges from the personal exploration of a dream is based on the dreamer's inner knowing. Dream insights can release a dreamer from reactive defensiveness, offering new, more positive ways forward.

USING WAKING FANTASY TO CONTINUE THE DREAM'S SCRIPT

Continuing with the gun example, let's see how the dream can be progressed by using the imaginative process of waking fantasy.

So what happens next? Remember this is your dream, you created it and you can carry it on to its completion. It is simply providing you with an opportunity to write your own scenario. Imagine you are in the dream now. How do you feel every time you go to the fridge and see the gun there?
"I feel angry."

So if you continued the dream now, what would you do with the gun?
"I'd put it under lock and key somewhere I don't go very often – perhaps the garden shed."

OK, do that. How do you feel with it tucked away in the garden shed?
"I still know it's there but I'm not constantly looking at it. I'd have to walk down the garden and unlock the door to get at it, so I'm less likely to spontaneously get into a shoot-out."

How does that apply to your work situation? How can you use this script you've created to stop you shooting your mouth off?
"I could avoid him, I suppose – not go where I know he'll be mouthing off."

What about when he comes to you?
"Well, I can't avoid him completely, but as long as I do my job and don't give him any cause for complaint, I should be all right. In fact, just talking about this makes me feel different… somehow the problem seems not quite so big."

Tell me who this chap at work reminds you of.
"I don't know really."

Think about the feeling you get when you're around him. When did you last feel that? Is it a familiar feeling?

"Yes, it is an old feeling, one I thought I'd got away from. It reminds me of when I was at school. I was just a lad from the village and there were all these toffee-nosed know-it-alls. [Sadly] *My brother became one of them."*

So these feelings surface when the new guy is around? Look at him and see him for who he really is. Remind yourself that you're not a little lad any more.

"Yes, I hadn't realized that. Poor bloke – he's just doing his job and I want to pile into him like I wanted to pile into those lads and my brother way back then."

Dealing with feelings that arise from dreams

Dreams are full of feelings – that's one of the reasons they have such an impact on us. In previous chapters we have demonstrated how feelings within a dream indicate that you need to pay attention to some aspect of your life. In fact, it could be said that the whole basis of dreaming rests on unresolved thoughts and feelings. Feelings do not go away: they need to be expressed, not only in order to make things happen, but also to forge a passage for the healing that can follow after their release.

Dreams provide you with a safety valve. Through your feeling-filled dreaming you can release tension and empty out the store of unexpressed emotion that has accumulated from constantly stuffing away responses you judge to be unacceptable, dangerous or even just uncomfortable. Feelings continually arise within you, and the more you withhold them, the more pressurized and inappropriate their expression becomes. As with anything under pressure, feelings become distorted and unrecognizable the longer they are denied. The bizarre images and ugly scenes in dreams often come from feelings you believe to be unspeakable. If faced and worked with, more often than not they turn out to be less dangerous and shaming than you had thought.

Dreams are the repository of your unfinished business, and their job is to sort, recycle and empty your emotional wastebin. They are doing this whether you pay attention to them or not. If you have filled yourself too full with unexpressed feelings, you might need to engage with your dreams in order to clear out your emotional blockages. Nothing is wrong – in fact, everything is working fine. You are just being nudged into re-evaluating the difficulties within your life and encouraged to find more creative solutions.

Frequently asked questions

WHAT IF I CAN'T REMEMBER MY DREAMS?

Everyone dreams and everyone can learn to remember their dreams (see Chapters 2 and 7 on dream recall). If, after trying the suggestions there, you are still unable to remember anything, you might want to conduct a dialogue with your missing dreams. This process is similar to the way we converse with dream characters. For example:

"Dreams, where are you? Why won't you come to me?"
Trust their answer. If they say they don't know, then translate that into gestalt terms, namely, "I won't tell you." Keep dialoguing. Of course, this is actually a conversation with the part of yourself that is resistant to accessing your dream world, so expect some difficulty.

"I want to know about you. I feel I'm missing out, that you are important. I really want to know what you're like."
You might find it useful to have this conversation in a telephone consultation with a member of our dream-catching team (see page 186). By asking the right questions, they might enable you to get in touch with why your dreams are escaping you. Below are some typical answers "non-dreamers" have evoked from talking to their absent dreams.

"You don't really want to know me because you'd have to change your life if you listened to me."

"I've stopped coming because you never listen to what I tell you."

"You're too busy and don't make enough time for me."
(This dreamer recognized the truth of this and decided to make more time for herself each morning during her holidays in order to get into the habit of recording her dreams.)

"I do come to you, but you get up and going in your life too quickly, so you forget me."

WHY ARE MY DREAMS ORDINARY AND INSIGNIFICANT?

That's what you think! Look at the loaf of bread dream in Chapter 5 and see what can be got from a dream fragment. Even the most mundane dream has meaning for your life. It might be challenging you about how boring you feel your life is, or telling you that you need some peace and quiet. There could be any number of messages within your dream that will become apparent only when you relive the dream in the present.

Work through all the images. You might have overlooked an "insignificant" part that holds a clue to the way forward. Through free-association you can tap into your imaginative dreaming process when you are awake. All you need is one image. When described, fully identified with and put into context, it will yield significant insights for you. Focus on the context around this image. Ask yourself where it comes from, what purpose it has or what it requires. Answers to questions like these may not at first surface easily. Trust that if an image flickers in front of your mind's eye it will have some useful connection to your dream work. Respect it and immerse yourself in it, even use it as a starting point for a waking dream. You will eventually tap into your dream's message.

WHY ARE MY DREAMS SO BIZARRE?

Dream imagery is a powerfully creative force. No matter how bizarre your dreams may appear, they will come to make sense if you relate to them through the dream-catching process (see the red octopus dream in Chapter 4). Most of us are quite proud of our unusual or weird dreams: instinctively we know we have created something marvellous. Look at any paradoxical circumstance in a dream as if it has its own rhyme and reason and eventually all will become clear. Using ordinary association and listening to how you describe and relate to the bizarre dream images will help you to decipher your dream symbols. The bizarre nature of a dream has a purpose. It might make us look anew at a familiar object, or search in our hearts and minds for how we are contorting the truth.

WHY DO I KEEP REMEMBERING AN OLD DREAM?

Long-remembered dreams hold significance for you now. It may be that you are now living through circumstances similar to those in the past. Or perhaps you are in a time of transition and the desire to move on and make changes could be stimulating memories of previous changes. Unfinished business from the distant past sometimes surfaces in the present. The important thing to remember is that you are now older and wiser, so you can do things differently. Memories of your old dream could also be reminding you to learn from the past, or perhaps you are being prompted to make your peace with a previous experience. Work with this old dream just as you would with any other. See if you can recall what was happening to you back then. Can you now see with hindsight what you needed to address then? Ask yourself what connections these insights have for your present situation. Are you now willing to make room for a new perspective or to try out a different approach?

Veronica, a middle-aged woman, had a dream that she had previously dreamt in childhood. She was in a room with boxes continually arriving and crowding her out. She described the room as a place to accommodate people, and recognized that that was what she did all the time; she liked to do that. However, she wanted to say to these boxes:

"Get out, give me space to breathe."

When asked how she would feel if she were given more space in her life, she said:
"That would be lovely; that would be heaven! We were crowded when I was a child. It's funny how the dream still applies."

Sometimes we create situations similar to past experiences in an attempt to manage them differently this time round. Our dreams also re-run important unfinished issues. Listen to your old dream. What must you do differently now? How would things change for you if you did take the risk of behaving in another way?

HOW CAN I MAKE SENSE OF MY DREAM WHEN I GET STUCK?

Any place you get stuck is significant. Go there and fully explore all of your associations with it and any accompanying feelings. How do you feel as you do this? Tense? Relaxed? Frightened? Sad? Is there anything you need to say when you are in this position? What support do you need?

Sometimes we find it difficult to ask directly for help. What would happen if you just stayed stuck? Notice your feelings and sit with them for a while.

What is it you are avoiding by trying to move on? Ask yourself what is on the other side of the sticking point. If you weren't stuck, what would you do? Can you think of anyone who might handle this situation in a better way? What would they do, and do you have any objections to behaving that way yourself? Can you think of any benefits in being stuck at this moment? For example, does it mean that you don't have to climb a mountain, cross an ocean or negotiate a slippery slope?

It is always useful to work a dream with someone else. This is even more true when you get stuck. Another person sees things from a different perspective and can invite you to look again at various possibilities. Others notice things that you avoid or skip over. They can hear your voice when it drops or gets excited. If your friend is also a dream-catcher, all the better. Every dream points to a solution. If you continue to be puzzled, telephone the Dream Catchers' helpline (see page 186) for an expert to work with you. You will be asked questions that will help you to access your dream's message more fully.

WHY DO I FEEL TOO AFRAID TO LOOK AT MY DREAM IN DETAIL?

There is probably something going on in your real life that you are also unwilling or too afraid to look at. It is important to get some assistance. Bad dreams are never as horrific as they seem. Facing the facts of our lives can be difficult, but do we really have an option? Sooner or later you will have to look, and sooner is always better because it usually offers more options. Some people believe that the arrival of a dream coincides with an individual's ability to deal with it.

Impartial assistance could help you to find the value in your dream, so seek out a fellow dreamer or a professional dream-catcher (see page 186). The support of another person's expertise can usually help you find the best way forward. The worry of not knowing or the anticipation of difficulty can make problems seem mountainous because fear feeds on itself. You need to ask, "If I loved myself, what would I do in these circumstances?" Call for support.

WHY DO I WAKE UP SCREAMING AND FRIGHTENED WHEN I CAN'T RECALL DREAMING?

Something is disturbing you and you could do with looking at your life past and present to see what you are struggling with. Take some time to evaluate the current stresses and strains of your life. What is your level of fear in everyday life? If you were to live your life being true to yourself, what would you need to change or confront, and what impact would that have on those around you? If you were to kick up a fuss in your life, what would it be about? How often do you reach out for help or reassurance? Look at where you have come from and check if there is something in your past that is nagging at you. Are there people you need to speak to? Imagine what you would say to them.

You have survived life so far. Your fear is just a projection into the future of a situation that is now over and done with but is still lingering in your memory, inhibiting your way forward. You might need to find a ritual to enable you to let go of past difficulties. Sometimes it helps to write a letter to a significant other and then burn it. Similarly, burying a symbol of what you need to let go of can be helpful, especially if you can acknowledge both good and bad parts of the relationship. Think about what you need to address, then imagine yourself free of it. Give yourself time to do this.

A counsellor who attended a short course about counselling couples talked about how she would often wake in the night in a furious rage. Her feelings were so violent that she would punch and hit her husband and throw things around the room. She had no idea what these rages were about. Through the couples course she learned about the dynamics within relationships and was able to identify that she had been self-sacrificing for most of her adult life. She was rarely aggressive or assertive, always understanding and accommodating. Her dream time was the only time she could not control her self.

Once she had made the connections with what she was suppressing in her life, she had no doubt about what to do. She realized that she needed to stop sacrificing herself to family and clients. She began to notice how she would needlessly keep herself out of the picture during work and family life. As she started to speak up a bit and give herself more time and attention, the violent episodes faded away.

WHY DO I WAKE UP SOBBING FOR NO APPARENT REASON?

During times of bereavement and great stress, it is not unusual to wake up in tears. Although you might not remember the dreams that provoked them, they are helping you to process feelings that you might be finding it difficult to express in your waking life. When we are in the midst of coping with loss and hurt, essential healing continues during sleep, where we can let go more easily. Trust your sleeping/dreaming processes – they are striving for your health.

If your weeping puzzles you because there is nothing in your life you want to cry about, try asking your subconscious for a dream to clarify what is going on.

WHAT IF MY DREAM IS UNFINISHED?

Dreams may be interrupted for many reasons. Sleep may sometimes be disturbed by outside forces, or sleepers might stop their dreams because they are unconsciously resistant to the events that could logically follow. If you have woken from an unfinished dream and feel curious about its conclusion, use waking fantasy to carry it on in your imagination, trusting your first thoughts. Allow the images that present themselves to follow through to an ending. Have confidence in what you produce and then work with it. If you do not like the ending you have created, ask yourself what you would change if you could and what support you might need to make those changes. The dream may be warning you that if you carry on the way you are, you will face consequences you might not want to know about. Look at your revised solution and imagine the changes you would have to make in real life in order to gain such an ending. This creative ending could change your present path and help you to avoid any unnecessarily painful consequences. Remember that your dream is a visual representation in cryptic form of something you already know but haven't yet become conscious of.

If you're afraid of facing the next part of your dream, come up for air – you don't have to dive back into your dream. If, however, you are still interested, you can keep working in waking fantasy or with the support of a fellow dream-catcher.

Sometimes we wake ourselves even from pleasurable dreams, perhaps because we are afraid of breaking some taboo or old parental rule. If this happens, ask yourself if you normally feel you must inhibit your pleasure. Was it forbidden to fool around? Have you taken too seriously an old warning that high spirits will end in tears? Keep exploring your dream and associate with the possibilities it offers you.

Should you experience any difficulties, you can always contact Dream Catchers for help (see page 186 for details).

10

DREAM-WORKING
OPPORTUNITIES

"…learning to understand our dreams
is a matter of learning to understand
our heart's language."

ANN FARADAY

If you need to make a life-changing decision, you are advised to consult your dreams because no matter what your head may be saying to you, your dreams will go straight to the core of the matter. If your unconscious processes are not taken into account, your best-laid plans are open to self-sabotage. Remember that your unconscious stores and sorts a great deal of information that you have been too busy to deal with when you are awake. It also holds intimate records of how you are and what is important for you. This information can become available to you through your dreams. Not tapping into your dreams at decisive periods in your life is like deciding to buy a car without a test drive. It makes sense to access all the information available to you before making a decision.

As you embark on your dream-catching journey, don't forget that support from the Dream Catchers organization is always available. Roland, a well-respected company director, contacted us when he was at a turning-point in his career. He was being head-hunted by several agencies and looked set for the last climb to the top. However, he was feeling increasingly disillusioned with the machinations of big business, and distinctly jaded by his work encroaching on time he wanted to spend with his wife and children. He had decided to take a break and review the options available to him. Now that he was feeling fit and refreshed, he was asking himself some questions.

Was it possible to invest his energy and finances in a way that could allow him to retain enough of his nourishing family base?

"I've just got back into good physical and mental shape. I have a beautiful life – tennis, great holidays, good chats with my wife, no shadows. I'm enjoying myself, not spending a lot of money. Everything's perfect. Now where I get confused and emotionally stirred up is when I ask myself 'What next'?

"A few months ago I wrote down how I would like things to shape up, what I'd love to do, and it happened. I had a good discussion about the possibilities with colleagues, everything looked set. I came back home late that night, went to the fridge for a glass of milk and was overtaken by sadness. I thought, 'I don't want this [his happy time at home] to be over so soon.' I don't want to make a mistake by running into something too quickly. I would hate to lose what I have now. I haven't had enough of it yet.

"What I had envisaged was a part-time job that wouldn't take all my energy. I want a job in order to live, not to live in order to do my job. Everything I have explored so far wants 150 per cent of me. I know that I need to re-enter work within six months to a year, before my sell-by date is up. But the more I live the way I want to, the more I feel that to go back would be to sell myself out. There are two partners who want me to join them in a new consulting business, but they refuse to hear that I want time with my family: they want 100 per cent of me.

"I went to a small recruitment agency just to see what they would say if I were absolutely honest about what I want and they said they couldn't sell me on those terms. It seems that if I don't sell my soul, they won't sell me. I feel like an alien in the culture. I'm good at my job, everybody wants me, but no one will negotiate on the hours. I don't even want the huge salaries any more, just enough to tick over.

"I've thought of three options for me: consultancy work, opening a bookshop, or retraining to help others. Perhaps all this is too grandiose and I'm seeking something that doesn't exist."

He asked for a dream and this is what he got.
"The whole family is bathing in a big, dark ocean. We are playing a ball game. I can see something, a big shape moving under water and I'm afraid that it's a shark. Then I see that it's a marlin. It tell the family that they don't have to be afraid, that it's only a marlin."

Be the ocean.
"I am vast, deep and cold. I have some darkness, not threatening, but I can be threatening. I can support some ball games and you having a nice time, but there are things in me that are dangerous."

Are you like this, Roland?
"Oh, yes, very! This is me."

Be the marlin.
"I am a big fish [laughs]. I've got a long nose. I'm very very fast and nobody is going to catch me. I'm self-sufficient, hunting alone, not aggressive, just enjoying life. I'm jumping around and just hunting for

my personal needs. There's a shoal of us having fun and playing around."

What would Roland's wife say about this situation?
"I am very confident in Roland. He put us into this deep ocean and I believe him when he says there is no threat. It feels a bit adventurous; it could be dangerous."

How do Roland's children feel?
"We're not bothered about anything. We just feel safe playing around."

Carry on as Roland in the dream.
"I was just playing around and then I realized that the ocean was quite dark and could be threatening. I had forgotten about this."

Be the ocean.
"Never forget that I can kill you. I can be powerful. I can destroy you."
[As himself] *"That's the reality of life. That's what kept me going for the past fifteen years: 'If you're doing the right thing, then I might allow you to play, to have two hours of fun.' That's the Baltic Sea for you!"*
[To the ocean] *"I would really prefer that you were the Mediterranean."*
[Sternly, as the ocean] *"You are on the Baltic Sea, my boy, and you need to swim here."*
[As himself] *"I hate to hear this. I hate that someone can tell me this. I'm getting really, really angry."*
(Roland was actually calm and mild-mannered, and only now, as all his years of kowtowing to the company came to mind, did he let go of his diplomatic charm.)

What's the difference between the Baltic Sea and the Mediterranean?
"The Baltic is tougher, cold and rough. While it has nice days, it has a long winter. It's much more life-threatening, and it's not nourishing unless you fish it. It doesn't support playfulness for man. This represents the whole working condition for me. I'm a northerner. How do I get a means of support that doesn't kill me? That's it! I will not concede. I feel very angry. Bloody hell, I don't want this. It's not enough."

What does the Baltic say?

"Take it or leave it. Don't play around with me."

What could be the end of this story? Here we have this guy facing out to the Baltic Sea. What next?

"He's not willing to concede and the ocean will kill him. I can't create a happy ending, going off to an island or something. This is the way it is. If he doesn't want to do it the way the ocean demands, the ocean will not make a concession. Part of me recognizes that even to try to negotiate is suicidal. I'll get swallowed up. There's a very big part of me that says, 'This is enough. I am not negotiating.'"

Through working his dream, Roland had now got the message that trying to negotiate a position in big business that would allow him what he wanted was not only difficult but probably impossible, and somewhere deep down he did not want to do it. He hadn't realized before how angry he was about the past fifteen years of self-sacrifice. He went on to look at another dream that seemed to offer him a different, more user-friendly option in a "fun store", but its message was essentially the same: he must work to replenish the stock-room that he had allowed to become depleted.

He was narrowing his options now, but was excited at having sounded the true note about his relationship to big business. He gave himself six months to work through to a realistic solution on a basis of honouring his needs, knowing his limitations and fighting for his priorities.

Now it's up to you

If you have read the book this far, you should now take one of your own dreams and work through it. You will be surprised with how far you can get by yourself. Once you get the hang of it, you'll be able to do a good deal of the groundwork for yourself, only needing to check with a friend or dream-catcher if you get stuck or have a question. Below are some of the different ways you can get support while you practise.

LECTURE DEMONSTRATIONS AND WORKSHOPS
One of the best ways to get to grips with the dream-catching process is to attend a lecture demonstration or workshop with an experienced dream-catcher.

In fact, you'll notice the benefits right from the first session. Each workshop begins with an explanation of the dream-catching process and an opportunity to ask questions. You will then be taken through a simple process that allows you to begin deciphering dreams for yourself. You'll be impressed with how rapidly your skills improve and how relevant your dreams are to your waking life. They will offer you new perspectives and new opportunities.

Our method of teaching is experiential, with theory being taught alongside "real" work. The material covered and the depth in which it is worked through depend on the interests and experience of the participants. A dream-catching weekend offers ample opportunities for you to work with dreams helped by a facilitator, a partner, or in small groups. A great deal can be learned through witnessing fellow participants working through their dreams.

A waking dream is used to introduce participants to the dream-catching process. The colour, texture and variety of the personal responses it evokes will clearly demonstrate how each person's id (the imaginative part of us that creates our dreams) uniquely makes sense of an experience. An individual's response to a dream reflects their particular concerns of the moment, as well as graphically demonstrating their way of being in the world. The varied responses of participants to the same story illustrate that the way we perceive the external world is intimately connected to our inner concerns.

During the working through of the waking dream, these individual differences become even more apparent. The dream-catcher will demonstrate how to work with the images and symbols presented by the group, delving as deeply or as lightly as participants feel comfortable with. The shared intimacy of this working through is intense, even within a group of strangers. Witnessing such private disclosures is a powerful experience, and each participant will respond in their own way to the poignancy, creativity and emotion that may be released within them while a waking fantasy or dream is explored.

Every dream is a story unfolding, each unravelling a revelation. When worked through, a merely interesting dream acquires a depth of meaning that can be profoundly moving. The dream-catcher may seem to take intuitive leaps and bounds, but all their actions are informed by years of experience and an intimate knowledge of the logic of the dreaming process. They work in close coordination with the dreamer in a way that may seem like magic to an inexperienced observer.

The energy liberated in an individual through the recognition of home truths is remarkable. Sticking-points can dissolve and relief becomes tangible, enabling fear to be replaced by self-esteem. At times sweetness and anger may sit alongside each other, and at others comedy may run high. The unfinished business of old hurts may surface and then fade into quiet contemplation as new perspectives open up new possibilities. Within the group each listener contributes their attention, willing the dreamer on and supporting them through the labyrinth of their dream. The goodwill and enthusiasm of fellow participants can enable a dreamer to release old patterns of behaviour and begin to expand into the vitality of the present moment.

Dream-catching in groups is inspiring and fascinating, and there is a lot to absorb. Some workshops offer a taping service so that you can record your working and go over the dream-catching process step by step at your leisure. It can be learnt by anyone who is willing to experiment and practise. The more dreams you work with, alone or with others, the more familiar you will become with the process. Your consciousness will expand as you become more aware and better able to access the deeper levels of meaning which will move you on to where you need to go.

Using the collective unconscious

Jung defined the collective unconscious as "the shared possession of all mankind, from which we can derive energy and wisdom". Even within the span of a weekend workshop, you will come to recognize the workings of the group unconscious as it evolves and manifests through group themes and individual symbols. Within just two days you can experience how each individual's dream issues are connected by a common thread informing and unravelling the dream messages. Over time, the collective unconscious process of a group will become even more apparent, and dreamers will grow in their awareness of both the individual and social interactions present in the group. Each group is a microcosm of society at large, as well as a mirror of family dynamics, and these reflections of external and internal reality can be used to help the dreamer break old, self-defeating patterns and experiment with different ways of relating.

In order to benefit from a workshop, it is not essential to have previous dream-working experience, but you do need an interest in the meaning of your dreams and a willingness to explore your motivations. Those who have already started to work with their dreams will gain from this opportunity to

enhance their dream-working skills. The level of integrity and goodwill within dream-catching groups is refreshing and stimulating, encouraging individuals to listen to themselves in a different way.

LONG-TERM GROUP WORKING

An effective way to consolidate your learning is to join an on-going dream-catching group. Initial meetings usually take the form of a day or a weekend foundation workshop, and thereafter on a weekly, fortnightly or monthly basis.

Over time the members of an on-going group will become familiar with the dream processes of the other participants, as well as their own. Each dreamer's contribution adds to and becomes part of the developing group culture. It is through this common experience that the group is able to evolve into a highly skilled team, working ever more subtly and efficiently to help its members uncover their dream messages. All participants are supported and challenged to recognize and work through their recurrent life themes and tasks. Dream-catching alliances and firm friendships form, enabling each person to develop the skills they will need to continue dream-catching once the group has ended. Some participants go on to study for the two-year dream-catching diploma, while others choose to stay another season for the camaraderie of the regular group meetings. All will be enriched by the experience.

RESIDENTIAL COURSES

From time to time Dream Catchers holds residential dreaming events where the culture of the workshop revolves around dream-sharing and dream-catching. The day starts with a dream circle and concludes after supper with creative entertainments. Participants are given the opportunity to practise their skills with each other under the guidance of a senior dream-catcher.

These events attract people from every walk of life. Some participants use these workshops as retreats where they can consult their dreams in order to clarify their options and find the best way forward. Others take the opportunity to develop their creative talents, using their dreaming as a base for artistic, dramatic and even technical creations. In such an environment dreams usually come freely, and participants leave the workshop satisfied, revitalized and confirmed in their life tasks. At times the aftermath of a powerful dream can cause the dreamer to feel vulnerable, not quite themselves (when in fact they are becoming more themselves). Dreamers are supported and encouraged to practise their newly discovered dream insights with group members in "real time". This gives them the opportunity to experiment and settle into new ways within a safe environment.

Residential workshops are usually held in the countryside, sometimes in France, where the beauty and tranquillity of the environment has strong restorative powers. For those wanting to train to work with the dreams of others, these residential courses can be credited towards the Cambridge GATE – Gestalt Awareness Training and Experience – dream-catching diploma, a two-year modular course for trainees with previous experience of counselling, therapy or dream-catching work.

INDIVIDUAL SESSIONS

Dream Catchers also offers opportunities for those who prefer to work with their dreams individually. Face-to-face sessions have the advantage of showing body language and expressions, but it is remarkable how well feelings can also be picked up during a telephone session.

The whole idea of this book is to give you the wherewithal to work on your dreams alone. Simply follow the steps in Chapter 4, consult Chapter 9 if you hit any problems, and contact us for support if you get stuck (see page 186).

ONLINE DREAM-CATCHING

While Internet consultations lose some of the immediacy of face-to-face work (even when videocams are used), the collective unconscious still operates within virtual groups. It is fascinating to see group themes evolving across the globe. An individual consultation online can provide an effective dream-catching session and offer suggestions for you to continue working on by yourself or with online interaction. Video conferencing and chat rooms for dream-catching trainees offer dream-catchers worldwide the opportunity to exchange their dreams and work with each other. Dream Catchers offers interactive dream-catching courses on the Internet for those unable to attend face-to face-training, as well as for those who wish to keep in touch or troubleshoot their dreams in between training or group sessions.

To contact Dream Catchers about any of the courses or opportunities described in this chapter, see page 186.

HELP FROM DREAM CATCHERS

Telephone us

If you want immediate support, call our **Dreamline 0906 734 0906** (8.30 a.m. – 9.30 p.m., UK only) and one of our qualified dream-catchers will work with you on your dream. This is a premium line, but just one session is usually enough to lay any ghosts or coach you through a sticking-point. To arrange a longer appointment call (UK) **0207 697 0029**. (Non-UK residents should contact us using one of the methods below for details of the telephone service in their area.)

E-mail us

Write to us at **dmail49596@aol.com** and we will send you information about the Dream Catchers organization and its programme of events. You might also like to e-mail us your dreams. This type of distance working is limited, but can be useful as a focusing aid. Personal follow-up sessions can be arranged, if necessary.

Visit our website

www.catchadream.net is designed to give you access to whatever dream information you need. You can interact with a waking dream from our library, post a notice on our bulletin board, chat with dreamers worldwide, or just troubleshoot your dreams. We offer online consultations, on-going groups and a variety of dream-catching courses, plus regular opportunities to link up with fellow dream-catchers. You will also find information about the best dream-related books, products and websites on the net.

Meet us face to face

Dream Catchers holds regular lecture demonstrations and workshops in the UK and occasionally overseas (see Chapter 10 for more detail about these sessions, and see above for contact details). These sessions, in plain language, teach people how to work on their dreams, but also offer help to those wanting to sort out a particular dream. We can also arrange individual sessions with local dream-catchers for UK residents.

Free newsletter

For readers who would like to keep abreast of dream-catching developments or find a dream buddy or dream group in their area, our free newsletter is available by e-mail (worldwide), or ordinary mail (EU residents only). Readers are invited to contribute by sending us examples of significant dreams they have caught, as well as any dream-related letters, articles or artwork. We are always interested in your feedback, so please feel free to contact us if you have any ideas or questions.

**Dream Catchers, PO Box 21406, London N1 0WS, United Kingdom
Telephone: +44 (0)20 7697 0029**

FURTHER READING

Dreaming

Bulkeley, Kelly, *The Wilderness of Dreams: Exploring the Religious Meanings of Dreams in Modern Western Culture* (State University of New York Press, 1994)

Carskadon, Mary A., *Encyclopedia of Sleep and Dreaming* (Macmillan, 1992)

Cunningham, Scott, *Sacred Sleep: Dreams and the Divine* (Crossing Press, 1992)

Empson, Jacob, *Sleeping and Dreaming* (Faber and Faber, 1989)

Faraday, Ann, *The Dream Body* (Berkley, 1997)

Garfield, Patricia, *The Healing Power of Dreams* (Fireside, 1991)

Lewis, James R., *The Dream Encyclopedia* (Visible Ink Press, 1995)

Mackenzie, Norman, *Dreams and Dreaming* (Vanguard Press, 1965)

Mircea, Eliade (ed.), *The Encyclopedia of Religion* (Macmillan, 1989)

Tedlock, Barbara (ed.), *Dreaming: Anthropological and Psychological Interpretations* (School of American Research Press, 1992)

Van de Castle, Robert L., *Our Dreaming Mind* (Ballantine, 1994)

Jung

Jung, C.G., *The Archetypes and the Collective Unconscious* (Princeton University Press, 1965)

Jung, C.G., *Memories, Dreams, Reflections* (Vintage Books, 1965)

Jung, C.G., *Man and His Symbols* (Picador, 1978)

Freud

Freud, Sigmund, *The Interpretation of Dreams* (Avon, 1965)

Freud, Sigmund, *On Dreams* (W.W. Norton, 1952)

Richman, John, *A General Selection from the Works of Sigmund Freud* (Doubleday, 1957)

Gestalt

McKewan, Jennifer, *Developing Gestalt Counselling* (Sage, 1977)

Perls, Frederick S., *Gestalt Therapy Verbatim* (Gestalt Journal Press, 1992)

Perls, Frederick S., *Gestalt Therapy – Excitement and Growth in the Human Personality* (Gestalt Journal Press, 1977)

Starak, Bernet, McLean, *Grounds for Gestalt* (Foreground Press).

Zinker, Joseph, **Wilde**, David, *Creative Process in Gestalt Therapy* (Vintage Press,1978)

General

de Bono, Edward, *Lateral Thinking* (Penguin, 1990)

Rimpoche, Sogyal, *The Tibetan Book of Living and Dying* (Rider, 1992)

Wilhelm, Richard (ed.), *I Ching or Book of Changes* (Arkana, 1997)

INDEX